ACKNOWLED

GW00493857

I should like to thank Maggie Bollaert and
Anne Marie Sjöholm of Plus One Gallery for their
help and encouragement

First published in 2014 by
Plus One Publishing
91 Pimlico Road
London SW1W 6ND
www.plusonegallery.com
ISBN 978–0–9928816–5–8

Enquiries: kmaclean@waitrose.com

Nicholas and Tece

SIR JOHN HAWKWOOD

English Knight and Florentine Hero
c.1320-1394

Love

Katie

KATHERINE MACLEAN

CHAPTERS

c.**1320** born Sible Hedingham Essex

1340 joins Edward III's army

1346 Battle of Crécy, France

1348 the plague breaks out in Europe

1356 Battle of Poitiers Knighthood conferred

1360 Becomes a mercenary Peace of Brétigny; leads advance on Avignon

1362 Pope Innocent VI dies and is succeeded by Urban V

1363 Arrival in the Italian peninsula

1364 First military assignment on behalf of Pisa versus Florence

1365 Transfers to the employment of the Visconti

1368 Wedding of Duke of Clarence with, Violante, daughter of Bernabo Visconti

1371 Pope Urban V dies and is succeeded by Gregory XI

1372 Transfers allegiance from the Visconti to the Papacy

1374 Breaks contract with the papacy and becomes freelance

1375 Mission in Umbria on behalf of the papacy

1375 Siege of Faenza

1376 Siege of Cesena Turning point in allegiance to the Pope

1376 Edward III dies in June

1377 Richard II accedes to English throne

1377 Joins Florentine Alliance Wins a Visconti Bride, Donnina

1378 Religious upheaval and birth of the Schism

1378 Pope Gregory XI dies and is succeded by Urban VI

1378 Election of Anti Pope Clement VII

1380 Appointed Captain General of Florence

1383 Campaigns in Naples

c**1385** Purchase of Castle of Montecchio

1387 Battle of Castagnaro

1389 Pope Urban VI dies and issucceeded by Boniface IX

1390 Florence attacks Milan at last . Hawkwood's final campaign

1391 Created Captain General for life and an honorary citizen of Florence

1394 Dies in Florence

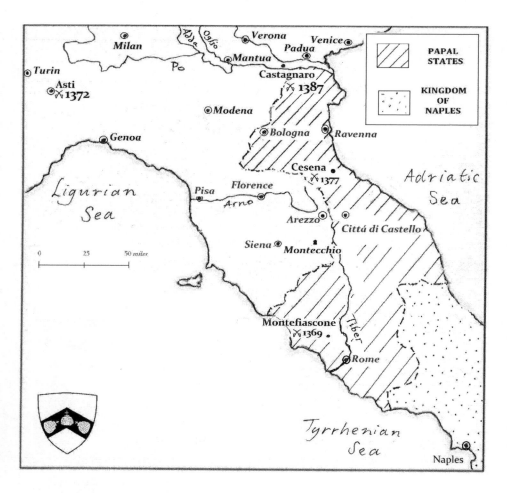

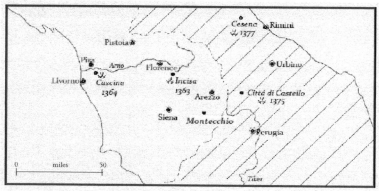

Northern Italy in the 14th century with a detail of Hawkwood's field of operation

PREFACE

Visitors to Florence who brave the queue to enter the Duomo, as the Cathedral of Santa Maria del Fiore is known today, may be surprised to find that the left-hand wall of the nave is dominated not by the usual familiar faces of revered Saints of the time but by two frescoes, each depicting an equestrian group. Both of them portray mercenary generals. Together they provide a stark and remarkable reminder of the importance attributed to military power in the Italy of the early 15th century.

More remarkable still the earlier of the two, executed and signed by Paolo Uccello in 1436, is identified by the inscription on the plinth as JOHANNES ACUTUS EQUES BRITANNICUS, DUX AETATIS SUAE CAUTISSIMUS ET REI MILITARIS PERITISSMUS HABITUS EST : [Johannes Acutus, English knight, the most circumspect leader of his age and its most skilled military strategist.] It is the city's noble monument to Sir John Hawkwood, an Englishman born around 1320 in Essex. and destined to a career as one the greatest of Europe's mercenary soldiers. The Anglo-Latin pun of "acutus" is a play on the Hawkwood 's name which was universally adopted in the peninsula, where he was known as "Giovanni Acuto".
The fresco is a trompe-l'oeil simulating a free-standing statue. Executed in a palette of green-grey against a vermilion background. with splashes of vermilion for the saddle and elaborate harness on the horse. It bears few signs that denote a

military hero. A sombre visaged rider, capped, cloaked and mounted on a heavy striding horse, wears no armour. His only weapon and the figure's only symbol of belligerence is a general's ceremonial staff carried in his right hand. The two humble coats of arms that decorate the plinth show only a black sable chevron and three argent scallops displayed against a white shield. Were it not for the grandiloquent inscription in the Latin of ancient Rome, implying the military status of a Caesar, the impression conveyed would be pacific.

If we wonder at finding this monument to a warrior inside a cathedral, so must have the Florentines of the day. It is the city's earliest memorial to a free condottiere – to give mercenaries their Italian name – ever to have been placed in a sacred setting; and, as the first documented equestrian portrait group known to have been created since classical times, it is also of art historical importance.

The fresco must also have been the inspiration for its neighbour in the Duomo, another equestrian group, dated over twenty years later and executed by Andrea del Castagno of the florentine general, Nicolo da Tolentino. This group must have set a precedent for the revival of equestrian statues which followed later in the 15th century.

The gothic masonry of the Hawkwood chantry built inside the english parish church of Sible Hedingham in Essex provides a striking contrast to the Hawkwood fresco in Florence. No queues here or tickets required, only the church key.

Carved against the south wall of the nave the arch of the chantry is decorated with hunting scenes showing the figures of hawks, the emblem of the Hawkwood family; boars, the emblem of Hawkwood's first patron John de Vere, Earl of Oxford; a pelican, symbol of self sacrifice and a fox, symbol of wisdom. The base carries a series of now empty shields, presumably originally emblazoned with the coats of arms of Hawkwood and of his companions.

Over the centuries the central fresco of the chantry has crumbled away. Fortunaely however, there remains a description from a local antiquary and dissenting minister, William Holman, who in 1715 describes how "painted in colour on the wall inside the arch was the figure of Sir John Hawkwood standing in devout posture with hands uplifted in prayer between his two wives, each figure with a prayer scroll coming from their mouths; Sir John's being *vere fili dei miserere mei* that of his first wife *[M]ater dei meme[n]to mei* and that of his second wife *[M]ater xi [Christi] meme[n]to mei*. The hand of the stonemason is unknown.

So what is it that Uccello and his patrons are trying to tell us? What in particular was it about Hawkwood, out of the many foreign mercenaries active in the peninsula, that decided the Florentines to immortalise him? What does the comparison between the two memorials tell us about the man?

This short book aims to outline the most notable of Hawkwood's achievements and to answer some of those tantalising questions.

An Essex childhood

John Hawkwood was born around 1320 in the English village of
Sible Hedingham in Essex during the strife ridden reign of
Edward II which ended with the King`s imprisonment and
murder at Berkeley Castle in 1327. Little is known of the family
but his father, Gilbert, must have been regarded as a member of
the local petty gentry of the time as Hawkwoods were recorded as
householders for at least two generations prior to John's birth.
Gilbert seems to have been a small property owner who could
well afford to keep his three sons, of which John was number
three, and four daughters.

Sible Hedingham dates back to Saxon times when its
name transcribed as 'the ham[let] of Hedin's people'. Sible could
possibly refer to a 13th century widow of a landowner of nearby
Laventon. The village lies eleven miles almost due north of what is
now the modern town of Braintree, quiet, sleepy and partially a
dormitory for London commuters. With little trace of its early
origins it is difficult to imagine that it was once reputed be the
second largest village in Essex. It's major industry, like so many
others in medieval times, was tanning.

The only remaining testament to the past is the church
perched on a hill above the present village. This was begun
around 1340 when John Hawkwood was about twenty and has
been much modified over the centuries.   A 14th century panel

above a window in the West Tower encloses a carved bird resembling a hawk, the Hawkwood family emblem as depicted on the later cenotaph inside the church. The family may well have subscribed to the building of the church and thereby gained recognition in the decoration.

The Hawkwoods were vassals and close associates of John de Vere, 7th Earl of Oxford at nearby Castle Hedingham. A man of enormous influence and wealth, de Vere was himself a close associate of the new King Edward III, and hereditary Lord Great Chamberlain of England. His extensive properties extended not only throughout Essex to Suffolk but also to Middlesex near London where his estate was in Cheniston, now known as Kensington, and included such sites as De Vere Gardens and Earls Court.

Castle Hedingham was built about 1140 for de Vere's ancestor, Aubrey de Vere, Archbishop of Canterbury, by William de Corbeuil. The Castle at the time ranked in importance and size with the Tower of London and Rochester Castle. Only the keep stands to day. Vast in size, the interior is supported by decorated arches in keeping with the status of the owner. Arches carved with decoration were reserved for use solely by people of high rank. The modern visitor is able to imagine something of the power and scale the former castle from the magnificence of this remaining fortification.

Looking out from the top of the keep towards the horizon the view dominates the countryside for miles around. Woebetide any enemy who dared to advance within eyeshot! As a small boy with his toy bow and arrow John Hawkwood must have been mesmerised by the hustle and bustle of the soldiers and their horses; the excitements of the periodic jousts and the tournaments which perhaps as a treat he was occasionally allowed to attend. It is not surprising that as he grew into manhood John is recorded as proving very proficient with the Longbow.

Little is known of John Hawkwood's childhood except what we glean from the 17th century diarist, Nicholas Jekyll, who indicates that he stood out amongst his contemporaries as a bright child with a taste for learning. Jekyll writes that *Young John showed himself a youth of pregnant parts & great hopes. on whom his father bestowed more Learning than was usual in those days of Ignorance; for besides reading & writing......he was instructed in the Rudements of Literature, & herein such was his Industry, that he exceeded his equals.*

With his passion for warfare Edward III encouraged the youth of the day to take part in longbow competitions, up and down the country, to the exclusion of all other sports in order to help create an efficient and enthusiastic generation of young militants to swell his armies. Edward was not the only leader in history to use these tactics and in the last century we may remember that Hitler used similar tactics in creating the Hitler Youth Movement. The French conversely were forbidden to carry arms, except in battle, and their young were in no way allowed to play with arms of any sort. This was a distinct political advantage to their bellicose neighbours across the Channel. The longbow was a weapon unique to England at the time. Normally made out of yew wood [yew trees can still be found growing in churchyards which would have afforded them some protection from robbers] but sometimes made from maple and oak, it was bent in an arc some six feet in length. It had an unprecedented range of 400 yards and could penetrate chain mail, it was also far lighter to carry than the heavy crossbows used on the continent. unlike to-day the English kept the secret of this weapon of relative mass destruction to themselves rather than try to market it around the world! It was largely due to its use that they so brilliantly trounced the French against all odds in the battle of Agincourt in 1415, almost 70 years after Crécy.

Captain at Crécy

In 1340 Gilbert Hawkwood died and left John, as a third son, no land but his keep by his elder brother for a year; 5 bushels of wheat; 5 bushels of oats; a bed and 20 pounds and a hundred Italian soldi; in fact enough to give a young man breathing space. It is alleged that in his early manhood John had been apprenticed by his father to a tailor in the City of London. Although there is no evidence to this effect, it is quite likely that he had been sent to London to learn the rudiments of some trade. However with his father's death and, by now 20 years old, John was free to choose his own career. Growing up in the shadow of Castle

Hedingham, and endowed with a notable prowess at manipulating the longbow, it is not surprising that he had developed a childhood longing to be a soldier in the king's army. His influential neighbour and patron, the elderly John de Vere, 7th Earl of Oxford, is likely to have noticed his promise and John would have had little difficulty in persuading de Vere to accept him into his regiment as a private soldier. It was thus that he received his entrée into the world of arms.

Around this time John married. Little is known of the identity of this his first wife but legend has it that she was Antiocha, one of de Vere's illegitimate daughters. The two families were certainly very close as witnessed by the fact that John's elder brother was named as executor of de Vere's will. John himself was a contemporary and fellow soldier of Thomas, the 8th Earl, in whose company he went to battle and the old Earl might well have entrusted one of his daughters to John's care. There is no recorded confirmation of this marriage, but evidence of its fruit lies in the known existence of three daughters, Antiocha, Fiorentina and Beatrice. There is also a mysterious reference to two, possibly natural, sons who accompanied their father to Italy and were imprisoned in Bologna in 1376.

What history was to name The Hundred Years War against France had just begun in 1337. Its initial cause was Edward's claim through his mother Isobel, daughter of Philip IV of France, to the French throne – a claim that had been dismissed by the French in favour of his cousin Philip of Valois. This war was to rumble on till 1453. King Edward now at the zenith of his powers was anxious to recruit to his army as many able young men as possible to participate in these battles. John's timing could not have been better.

The 1340s and 1350s witnessed England's great victories against the French and Spanish most notably at Sluys [1340], Crécy [1346], Winchelsea [1350] and Poitiers [1356]. The long drawn out siege of Calais culminated in 1345, giving the English navy a harbour in a strategic position the other side of the Channel, and England the long sought after foothold on the continent, which it retained for 200 years – a coup in which Edward was to glory for the rest of his long reign.

By 1346 Hawkwood had risen through the ranks to be a Captain, and as such he fought in the famous Battle of Crécy, south of Calais, at which Edward's forces defeated those of Philip VI. At this battle, the first great English victory of the Hundred Years War, the English cornered the more numerous French against the setting sun and then, thanks to cunning strategies and their precious longbows, wrought havoc amongst the enemy. French losses in this bloody battle are estimated to be up to 10,000 compared to the 300 english casualties.

The 16 year old Prince of Wales, Edward Woodstock, later known as the Black Prince on account of his black armour, commanded the vanguard of this bloody battle, which at one moment appeared overcome by the enemy. The prince appealed to his father for help who at first showed little sympathy and sent the messenger back with the often quoted injunction "let the boy win his spurs". However Edward could observe from his vantage point on the summit that all was not well and had the heart, so we understand, to send Hawkwood and a few fellow officers to help the boy out. His strategy worked and the young Prince emerged the hero of the day. On the battlefield died, Johann, the blind King of Bohemia, who had gallantly, if foolishly, charged into battle led by his knights. At Johann's burial the Black Prince plucked from his palanquin the plume of ostrich feathers, which together with the motto "*ich dien*" has crowned the crest of all Princes of Wales ever since.

Edward staged a vast public relations exercise in recruitment to arms by many diverse means. For instance he encouraged the extravagant rituals of tournaments and other shows of military prowess throughout the country. He also re-established the cult of the Arthurian order of Chivalry, with its use of a round table for conferences at which no one person could be deemed to sit at the head.

In 1344 he created the Fraternity of St George. Next to Windsor Castle the king built a college and chapel for the order dedicated to St. George, whom he claimed as England's patron saint. The order was and remains the most prestigious order of English knighthood in the land. Shortly after its institution, so the story goes, whilst dancing with the king at a Windsor ball the Countess of Salisbury dropped her garter. With the manners of a true knight the king picked it up and placed it on his own leg commenting to those around "honi soit qui mal y pense" [shame to him who thinks evil of it]. Subsequently the order became known and survives to this day as the Order of the Garter.

By all these means Edward aimed to promote the glory of a soldier's life and mask the grim realities and probabilities of a bloody death which might await them.

Meanwhile Hawkwood was rapidly becoming a favourite and confidant of the king, who seems frequently to have sought his counsel on questions of military strategy and politics rather than that of his appointed statesmen. Despite England's great military successes, or perhaps resulting from them, these were economically testing times for Edward who was always short of the huge sums needed for wars. England was a largely agricultural country with vast areas of sheep farming producing an enormous output of wool, backed up by the tin mines of Cornwall and numerous coal mines. Minerals were not an easy commodity to export and Edward had thus to depend largely on the sale of wool on which he imposed a customs tax in 1343. One of his chief outlets was Florence where the local craftsmen were expert and talented weavers of cloth. His loans from the Florentine bankers Peruzzi and Bardi were reputed to amount to half a million pounds. Popular contemporary legend based largely on the writings of Matteo Villani – a relation of the Peruzzi bankers- accuses Edward of defaulting on repayment of much of his debt thus rendering many of his creditors, bankrupt. Subsequent research has proved that Edward's debts amounted to little more than £13,000 and that internal disputes were probably responsible for the collapse of these Florentine banks. Further support of this theory is the siultaneous collapse of the Acciaiuoli family bank, with whom Edward never traded.

The surest way to die

In 1348 Europe was struck with an incurable disease which was to recur at repeated intervals over the next fifty years. It took the form of a virus allegedly introduced to Genoa by ships importing spices from India infiltrated by a species of disease bearing black rats. The first symptoms were the appearance of swellings in the groin or armpit which spread all over the body accompanied by a high fever. No treatment seemed able to contain the virus. Like lepers, the victims were ostracised by family, friends and even doctors through fear of contagion. The corpses were flung into communal graves in the form of deep pits. The virus contaminated not only people but food and clothes. It was quickly spread by the primitive drains of the time. The stench was venomous. Food, already in short supply became shorter still, with the dearth of labourers to till the land. Local populations looked everywhere for a scapegoat. Some suspicion fell upon the already persecuted Jewish population many of whom fled, hiding their jewels and treasures as they left.

The devastation to town and country was beyond belief. Italy, wasthe first victim and particularly badly hit with outbreaks continuing until the end of the century. In Venice at least three quarters of the population died. In Florence the virus

raged for so long the it was known as "the plague of Florence".
It attacked in waves. In Siena, for instance, it raged from April to
October 1348 killing eighty thousand souls. A testament to the
impact of the disease on human progress is the truncated transept
of Siena Cathedral, where building work came to a halt. The
abrupt unfinished ends of many chronicles of the time, such as that
of the Florentine Giovanni Villani, also bear witness to the
devastation. The untimely death of the great sienese painters
Pietro and Ambrogio Lorenzetti cut short the development of
what might have become a great school of artists, and the city was
greatly weakened politically by the loss of so many citizens. The
disease was ruthless and showed no discrimination between rich
and poor, nobles and peasants, scholars and townsfolk. No-one
was secure.

The plague quickly spread throughout Europe as far north
as Germany and England where the death rate of the population
was calculated at between forty to fifty per cent. In East Anglia
alone the population was cut by half. The plague was so virulent
and long drawn out in England that it became a way of life and
was named the Black Death after the black blotches which
manifested themselves on the victims' bodies. The plethora of
magnificent medieval churches to be seen in East Anglia, many of
them now often looking out over empty fields, bear witness to
the numbers of parishioners whom they must have once served
which have never been regained. In Norwich alone 60,000
deaths were recorded and two thirds of the parishes left without
priests. The dearth of labourers to herd the sheep and cattle led to

the introduction of hedges to protect the animals. The psychological effect on those of the population lucky enough to survive was debilitating to say the least.

Battle spurs at Poitiers

From a political point of view it was fortunate for England that the plague had hit France as severely as herself. The common suffering and exhaustion forced both countries to an uneasy truce and a few years of calm. It was no time for reaping the fruits of Crécy.

Not until 1355 did the failure of a last effort to convert the truce into a final peace drive the English back into war. In the intervening years history had moved on. Pope Clement VI had died and been succeeded by yet another French Pope, Innocent VI. King Philip VI of France had also died and been succeeded upon his demise by his son Jean who, spurred on by a quarrel that had arisen between him and Charles the Bad, King of Navarre, appealed to Edward for help, tempting him with the promise of the large fiefs he held as a Valois in Normandy. Edward could not resist the opportunity to take up arms against the French once more. Held up by contrary winds, the invading English contingent never made the French shores. Charles, in despair, made peace with Jean only to find the French king a rogue, who did not keep his word but seized Charles, and executed his chief advisor. Edward was not deterred by one defeat and sent off a further contingent under the Duke of Lancaster whom King Jean managed to drive westwards to Cherbourg out of harm's way.

The French king had not reckoned with the arrival of the Black Prince in the south western province of Guyenne whence, he learned, the prince planned to head towards the Loire to meet up with Lancaster's force. His advance pointed straight towards Paris enforcing Jean to abandon all other plans and head down to the Loire to confront him. The English were unaware of the huge size of the French presence until they reached the fields north of Poitiers. There they found their line of retreat totally cut off by a french army estimated as numbering fifty thousand stretching as far west as Bordeaux. The English forces numbered in the region of a mere eight thousand. To all appearances the odds were loaded against them.

The Cardinal of Périgord anxious to keep the peace between his French and English neighbours – Aquitaine being an English possession at the time – rode up from the town of Poitiers and made several overtures to negotiate a truce between the French king and the English prince, whom he feared would be overwhelmed in any ensuing conflict. The Prince, aware of his position, was quite agreeable to co-operate if the terms were right. He is alleged by the french medieval historian Jean Froissart to have offered to surrender all the towns and castles he had captured during the recent campaign, to set free, all his prisoners, and to swear not to take up arms against the king of France for seven years. Despite these reasonable terms, the French king would not be satisfied with less than an unconditional surrender by the Black Prince of himself and of his army. The poor Cardinal was sent back ignominiously to Poitiers.

The Prince rising to the occasion exhorted his troops in the words recorded by Froissart:

" My gallant men, we are only a few against the might of our enemies, but do not let us be discouraged by that. Victory goes not to the greater number, but where God wishes to send it. If we win the day, we shall gain the greatest honour and glory in the world. If we are killed, there will still be the king my father, and my noble brothers, and all our good friends, to avenge us. I therefore beg of you to fight manfully today; for, please God and Saint George, today you will see me act like a true knight."

So battle commenced and the French advanced. Despite the paucity of their numbers the English did have one strategic advantage. They had made camp in a vineyard full of thorn bushes which were very difficult to penetrate. In order to attack the French needed to approach down a narrow lane where the high hedges on both sides were lined with English archers whose brilliant and deadly aim with the longbow disrupted their cavalry. Several horses were wounded, others panicked, bucking and throwing their riders and in the ensuing confusion became unmanageable. Chaos reigned. The French started to retreat only to be met by an English troop who had been held in reserve on a hilltop and now swooped upon the enemy's flank demolishing their opponents. The French had not bargained for the brilliant strategy of the young English prince in fighting a defensive battle against all odds. With a greatly inferior force he succeeded in inflicting casualties of up to 8,000 on the enemy, whilst sustaining only a few hundred on the English side.

King Jean finally surrendered and was treated with great courtesy by his young English cousin. A feast was given by the victors provisioned with captured french victuals to which all the captives were invited! Eventually King Jean was brought back to England. Mounted on a white charger, he was processed in triumph through London by the Black Prince on a little black hackney. and led to the Savoy Palace. He was lodged there in comfort for the duration of his captivity.

This completely unplanned battle at Poitiers was to go down in history as one of England's greatest victories. John Hawkwood, one of the English officers under the leadership of the 26 year old prince, distinguished himself on the battlefield sufficiently to be recommended by the prince to his father for a knighthood. This was indeed an honour for one who had come up through the ranks from relatively humble origins, and who lacked the financial resources which usually accompanied that position. No wonder that Froissart refers to him as "the poorest knight in the country."

Enter the Mercenary

May 8th 1360 was a red letter day for King Edward III. At Brétigny, a village south east of Chartres, he concluded a peace with the French by which he relinquished his feudal claim to the duchies of Normandy and Touraine, the counties of Anjou and Maine, and the suzerainty of Brittany and Flanders. Edward also renounced his claim to the french throne. In return he received several territories in an expanded province of Aquitaine and the all-important port of Calais. The acquisition of the latter at last afforded the English a harbour on the continent for their navy. The renunciation of sovereignty was written in a separate document, with the provision that the treaty was to be carried out by November 1361. This treaty did not lead to lasting peace, but it did procure a nine year respite for the English in the endless years of fighting. This was welcome to the English people who were tired of Edward and his wars and his ever-increasing demand for taxes.

For soldiers, such as Hawkwood, peace was a financial disaster. After seventeen years of hard military labour he found himself out of work and without an incomeKnights of his standing normally owned lands and had private resources, but Hawkwood was without capital or estates. He desperately needed work.

Ever resourceful, and with the blessing of his king, Hawkwood formed a company of freebooters drawn from fellow out–of–work soldiers. The agreement was that they would go plundering in France and place their profits at the disposal of the king, whose coffers had been emptied by the long years of war and were in dire need of replenishment. It would be harsh to judge Hawkwood's move as one of villainy. After all, he had the king's blessing; he was providing employment for otherwise jobless soldiers and the profits of his endeavours were to be declared and placed at the disposal of the Sovereign. Undoubtedly there would have been an arrangement by which those involved would receive payment out of these monies. As for the plundering of the french countryside, seen through the eyes of contemporaries, this was how armies operated. Unlike today when armies are paid out of the defence budget of their ruling government there were no regular wages for soldiers in work, let alone those out of work. Looting was regarded as legitimate recompense. Soldiers needed to fight to survive.

For all these reasons it was a good moment for Hawkwood to leave England. In addition a fresh outbreak of the Black Death had descended on the country. The repressive measures of Parliament and the landowners were widening the social chasm between employers and employed, sowing the seeds of civil unrest whose flames were fanned by the rabble rouser, John Ball, a mad priest from Kent.

The Road To Avignon

Late in1360, Hawkwood and his merry band set off through northern France marauding as they went. The invaders made their way south, following the Rhone towards te city of Avignon, seat of the papacy for the past 50 years. In December they captured the small town of Pont Saint Esprit some 25 miles north of the city. It was strategically placed on the Rhone at a crossing much used by pilgrims on their way to Santiago di Compostela in Spain. The town was also a centre for the corn, wine and salt trade and for the collection of taxes and tolls.

The papacy had been in voluntary exile in Avignon since 1309 when she was taken there by Pope Clement V.   Pope John XXII moved the papal seat permanently to this city and soon after his election in 1316 began work on the creation of the magnificent palace known as Le Palais des Papes. Under his successor, Clement VI, the city grew in size and wealth, attracting the leading jewellers, silversmiths and craftsmen of the day to the new Papal Court, as well as men of letters and the arts.

In 1361 the incumbent of that court was Innocent VI, the fifth in a series of seven French popes who ruled over the Catholic church from the comfort of their native land, and had established themselves in Avignon as a rival in power and riches to the French court. It was described by Ludwig von Pastor as *an extraordinary mixture of castle and convent, palace and fortr* ess.

On learning of the threat of Hawkwood's band bearing down on his precious stronghold Innocent was sorely afraid. However God and fate were on his side. The freebooters imminent arrival coincided with an appeal to the Pope by the Marquis de Montferrat in Piedmont for help against the invasion of his lands by the powerful Visconti of Milan. Seizing the opportunity Innocent approached Hawkwood with the attractive and cunning proposal of professional work across the Alps, combined with a hefty financial contribution towards expenses. By using the lure of good work and serious money His Holiness was able to rid himself of his unwanted guests and at the same time grant a favour to an ally.

Hawkwood allowed his comrades to cross the Alps without him. He had more important, or perhaps more lucrative, business to finish in France. Several units of free fighters, or "routes" as they were known, had clubbed together to fight a French force that was laying siege to the town of Brignais near Lyon, which they were using as their headquarters. The commander of the garrison was Hélie Meschin, somewhat of a character as he had once been a valet at the French court. This "Little Meschin", as he was known, had sent out an SOS to his fellow routiers, which brought assistance from far and wide. The French attackers were taken off their guard and suffered a bloody defeat in April 1362. Their commander Jaques de Bourbon was captured and killed. The loot and financial rewards were manifold which might have been a large part of the attraction.

Across the Alps

When Hawkwood rejoined his comrades in the Piedmont in 1363 he found they had allied themselves with the "tards venus" or latecomers, the nickname given to bands of soldiers operating in provinces already stripped bare, to fight for the pope on behalf of Montferrat under the german leader, Albrecht Sterz. This assorted band of brigands was highly successful, laying waste the Visconti territory in Piedmont. Moving on towards Milan they had finally managed to trounce the Visconti Hungarian troops at the bridge of Canturino near Novarra. The Hungarian commander Conrad Landau was mortally wounded on January 4th, 1363. Stricken by defeat and new outbursts of the plague neither side was in a fit state to profit from the outcome of the battle and finally a truce was reached between the Visconti and the pope. The reputation of the invaders, and of Hawkwood, had by this time travelled across the peninsula. Ambassadors from Pisa arrived at the English camp with attractive offers of employment.

It was thus that Hawkwood arrived in the land where he was destined to spend the next 30 years of his life until his death. At the then ripe age of 40 he was already an established and experienced soldier whose skills had been noted in European military circles. He was now an independent knight open to serve

which prince or cause would reward him most. By force-majeur
he had become a "condottiere", the Italian name for a mercenary,
who fought under the terms of an agreement called a "condotta".
This was the role into which Hawkwood unwittingly fell, only
differing from his international peers in that he never lost his
allegiance to the king of England.

Throughout the course of history mercenaries have had a bad
press, no less so in the fourteenth century when the Florentine
historian Matteo Villani wrote *their hands are venal and they turn*
themselves where they can find the greater gain... However wars
in the peninsula were fought almost exclusively by them.
There did exist a local system of military levy which could be
imposed, but this seldom produced skilled soldiers and the
imposition caused a great distraction to trade. Many cities found
it cheaper and more expedient to employ mercenaries, of whom
there was a plentiful supply from neighbouring European
countries, especially Germany. The Italian peninsula moreover
had been particularly badly hit by the plague where outbreaks
continued at regular intervals until the end of the 14th century
vastly reducing the population.

Italia! Italia!

It was only in the early 19th century with the onslaught of the French and Napoleon's attempt to instil a feeling of nationhood into the peninsula that the name of "Italy" for the conglomeration of all the city states in the peninsula began to be adopted in common parlance. The use of the name "Italians" for the population of the peninsula derives from *popolo italico,* the name of those people living in the Valle Padana, who occupied the territory north of the Tiber up to Emilia, and the central part of Etruria. In early history They were in territorial opposition to the neighbouring *popolo etrusci* living predominantly in Etruria, that part of modern Umbria lying to the west of the Tiber. The archaeological remains and artefacts left by these early neighbours show evidence of a more sophisticated, cultured, intellectual, and liberal lifestyle than that practised by the Romans. Such characteristics bore the influence of Greece and the other Mediterranean countries from which the Etruscans had emigrated. They were fortunate to find a plethora of raw materials in Etruria with which to continue creating the beautiful clay and bronze vessels at which they excelled, some of which luckily still exist to tell the tale. Although gradually supplanted by Rome it was not till the first century AD the Etruscans finally succumbed to her superior military strength and faded away.

By 1363 at a time when work was scarce in England, the northern states of the peninsula in which Hawkwood found himself was a paradise for mercenaries. The old nobility had been cut down in bloody civil wars only to make room for a new form of tyrants, the autocratic "*Signori Principi*". A nationalist concept no longer existed in the north and centre of the peninsula, which had lapsed into a collection of warring city states, all at loggerheads with each other. Conversely, the south of the peninsula retained its feudal structure and was united in the Kingdom of Naples, ruled over by the Angevin dynasty, whose leadership was hotly disputed by the French and Hungarians. The resulting confusion in the north left the field wide open to aspiring foreign mercenaries.

Emergent from this maelstrom were three major powers: Foremost was the papacy, which despite its exile to Avignon in 1316, after yet another sack of Rome by the barbaric Goths from the north, still held enormous sway over the peninsula where it held vast lands in temporal power. These lands had been handed to it in the 8th century when the then pope, Stephen III, had enlisted the help of the Franks under the leadership of King Pepin the Short to rid him of the menace of the lombard invasion in the peninsula. Having secured his reconsecration as King of the Franks, Pepin and his people rallied to the cause of St Peter, drove out the Lombards and handed the menaced territories over in sovereignty to the pope. Thus the papacy became a major landowner in the peninsula. Its lands were known as the Papal States corresponding to the modern regions of Emilia Romagna, the Marches, Umbria and Lazio were incorporated into the newly unified Italy in 1860.

By 1360 The grandiose palace initiated by Pope John XXII was complete. During the intervening years the papacy had created a wealthy cultural and artistic centre in Avignon to rival that of Paris. It attracted leading craftsmen and artists of the day, their ranks swollen by the number of artisans necessary to service the Papal Court. The city bustled not only with jewellers, furriers and other suppliers of luxury goods, but also with cabinet makers, tailors, dress designers, cloth merchants and, in particular, ironmongers who were greatly in demand to forge armour for all the knights. The fashions set in the papal court travelled not only through France but also over the alps to the Italian peninsula. Surrounding the pope were the leading clerics and scholars of the day, establishing the city as a centre of learning whose influence spread throughout Europe.

The papacy's most dangerous opponents, and the second great power in the peninsula were the Milanese Visconti against whom Hawkwood's band of freebooters had been lured accross the alps to help the Marquis of Montferrat. They were prolific in numbers, having largely escaped the death toll of the plague, and as such, immensely powerful.

The Visconti were adherents of the Holy Roman Emperor who were known as Ghibellines, deriving from the term "guidi belli." Their rivals were the followers of the pope, and consisted of a group largely composed of rich merchants who profited from the presence of the papacy in their midst. This group were known as Guelphs, a name deriving from the term "guidi la fede." These two political divisions sprung from the struggle for power between the papacy and the Holy Roman Empire which had been raging for over 200 years. The chief issue of debate between them regarded the "investiture" of bishops by the emperor who the pope claimed enjoyed secular but not sacred authority.

By 1360 when Hawkwood entered the peninsula the Ghibellines were largely represented by groups of fading aristocrats. The Visconti of Milan in Lombardy were the exception. Though not famed for their wisdom or valour they were notorious for their tyranny and love of pleasure. Their sporting activities such as boar hunting and shooting surpassed all others in Europe.

The leadership of the Visconti family devolved on two brothers Bernabo and Galeazzo. The latter was considered the handsomest man in Italy. He lived in Pavia, where he indulged his passion for books and built up the library bequeathed to him by his archbishop uncle. His literary advisor was no less than the famous poet, and important figure in the rediscovery of classical antiquity, Francesco Petrarch. It was not unusual at the time for warriors to harbour an appetite for literature and art. Being a collector of works of art was a manifestation of power and brought with it a social status. Galeazzo had the money and the curiosity to explore the pagan beliefs and classical texts of the Romans which were to inspire the early years of what was subsequently labelled "the Renaissance".

In political and military terms, Galeazzo was the junior partner to his brother, Bernabo, who was using the most brutal methods to extend the power of the Visconti over the territory of the papal states. Bernabo was both a great and ferocious warrior and a larger than life figure, at the same time kind, humorous and exasperating. He indulged in dozens of mistresses and sired scores of illegitimate children. His passion for the battlefield was rivalled only by that for the hunting field. He excelled on both. He is said to have inherited these talents, and characteristics, from his Doria ancestors from Genoa.

The third power to show its head in the 14th century was the Republic of Florence.

In 1333 the city had suffered from a devastating flood of the river Arno. Four days of non–stop rain and storms had caused untold harm destroying many buildings. The following year Giotto di Bondone, the painter and architect, had been commissioned to rebuild the destroyed walls of the city and to build a tower for their cathedral Santa Reparata. Bondone had appointed himself Captain of the Guard and Keeper of the Peace in the city state. With this position went the command of 50 knights and 100 footsoldiers for the maintenance of public order and the suppression of crime. Bondone was a good leader and in 1336 had made an alliance with Venice and Milan against Martino delle Scala, Lord of Verona. The following year he died.

He is more usually known to posterity as "Giotto", the first painter to carry Italian painting out of the iconic imagery of Byzantine art into a freer more naturalistic style, later taken up in the Renaissance.

Economically Florence began to prosper and a 1338 census numbered the population at 90,000, the highest of any city in Europe. Politically, however, it was not a happy scene. In 1342 a foreigner Walter de Brienne, known as the Duke of Athens had been handed over the reins of government. He only lasted a year before a popular revolt ended the experiment. In 1343, the Duke was expelled from the city and Florence established itself as a republic, governed by a single unit or family [Signoria] with a committee [Priori]. The newly formed city state prospered as a centre of manufacturers and exporters of woollen and silk cloth. The raw wool which they used was largely imported from England in return for huge sums of money, which Edward III demanded from the Florentine banks who had succeeded the Lombard and Jewish money-lending institutions. These banks were the first to issue bills of exchange. In 1252 they had introduced the fiorino d'oro or "florin", the onomatopoeic-named coin which became common currency until the 15th century when it was replaced by the venetian "ducat". It was perhaps natural that it was to these bankers, with whom he was already in business, that Edward III turned to raise large loans at the outset of the Hundred Years war. As a burgeoning centre of commerce Florence had established its capitalistic strength as the cardinal point of its politics. Then like now money talked.

Dante, banished from Florence due to his Ghibelline affiliations in 1267, had died in Ravenna leaving his great work, the Divine Comedy, completed but forgotten. However in the 14th century interest in his work had revived. By the 1350s the city had overgrown its tuscan neighbours. Trade flourished– in particular the making of textiles. The resulting wealth created opportunities for the pursuit of culture and banking. However, as so often happens in periods of opulence, the poor were exploited by the rich. Overcrowding and malnutrition were rife, giving way to disease fanned by a plague of rats, and riots.

In 1363 when Hawkwood arrived in the peninsula Florence, though independent of the Papal States, was allied to the papacy by what was called the the Guelphic Agreement. As such the city was in opposition to the Milanese Visconti who were Ghibellines and adherents to the Holy Roman Emperor.

Hawkwood was to work for all three of these powers and for his first fourteen years in the peninsula flitted from one to another as was expedient.

A foreign and exotic land

In the fourteenth century this peninsula was a world apart from
England. The population was double, despite the immense losses
of the plague. All the land was husbanded, the countryside of the
north was mountainous and bathed in sunshine for many months
of the year. The beauty and majesty of the surrounding
countryside must have astonished Hawkwood and his men after
the rolling and sometimes bleak Essex countryside.

In the peninsula trades of diverse forms flourished.
merchants from the whole of western Europe, from Venice to
Genoa, passed through the Po valley with their wares. The many
warring states were ruled by princes who often combined their
warlike traits with a love of culture. A banking system already
existed and Florence's florin was international currency.

England on the other hand, to quote Pope Pius II who
came from Siena, was:" *rude uncultivated and unvisited by the
winter sun.*" Her chief and only trade of any size was in wool,
which she largely sold to Italy. Although light industries such as
tanning and leather working were to be found in almost every
town they were only on a local scale. As an island, difficult of
access, little international passing trade existed. As a country she
lagged behind northern Italy in many ways including their
business practices, their thinking and their lifestyle. In the 1360s

the homes of most English soldiers were simple houses, made of
daub and watle, in small villages clustered around a stone built
church. The village streets were made of mud. The gentry lived
in half timbered houses. Whereas churches, castles and great
houses were made of stone, dwellings of the really poor were of
far humbler construction. At the time of the Black Death they
were often no more than primitive wooden huts constructed with
walls of sods, trampled earth or mud–plastered walls, the roofs of
unshaped poles covered with turf, heather or straw as described
by F.Salzmann. The writer quotesa contemporary description:"
*probably a third of the houses were wretched nastt cabins without
chimney, window or dore–shutt.*" The public streets were
narrow, crowded and filthy. The pig was ubiquitous, so was pig
dung. The population was divided into three categories: those
who worked the land; those who fought and those who prayed.
The latter comprised the many religious orders which lived in
relative comfort despite their vows of poverty.

An example of 14th century domestic architecture is the
Clergy House at Alfriston in Sussex, the core of which is a
Wealdon Hall House of 1350. Nestled close to the church of the
same date, the thatched house with half timbered outer walls, has
window frames of oak. Although the entrance doors are low,
denoting man's average height of the time, the inner hall is lofty.
It's wattle and daub walls have an oak dado with a moulded
finish.The floor resembling modern concrete is made of a
mixture of sour milk and chalk, of which there was, and still is,

an abundance in the neighbourhood. In the middle of the floor burned the fire whose smoke escaped through an hole in the roof.

In the piazzas of the Italian cities the citizens promenaded of a spring evening in lively exchange of ideas and news before returning to their stone built dwellings. In England stone was harder to come by, whereas wood was still in plentiful supply. In the peninsula wood was scarce and conversely only used by the rich. The difference in architecture between the two countries was largely influenced by the materials available, and of course the weather. However the poor fared no better in the peninsula than in England. For instance in Florence in houses, such as the Palazzo Davanzati, the servants slept in corners where they could find space. In the heat of the summer they slept in the street, which in the English climate would have been impossible.

What about their diet? The chief difference would have been in their drink. Whereas in England milk, ale and mead were plentiful, in the peninsula ale was unheard of and milk scarce and often unsafe. The chief drink in the peninsula was wine. Although Edward III received regular deliveries of wine from Bordeaux, it was a great luxury virtually unknown to the English soldier. As regards food the English diet would have been largely based on granary and dairy products, accompanied by vegetables in season such as onions, leeks, cabbage, turnips and parsnips with few frills. What might be called 'good plain cooking'.

In Italy, pre the days of pasta, the normal diet would have consisted largely of pulses such as beans and chick peas. Spinach, onions and leeks were indigenous. Meat was expensive. Fish was

39

popular where accessible. Pork would have been eaten up till lent and lamb as a special treat at Easter. Lacking wheat they made flour out of chestnuts which, in all forms, were part of their staple diet. Tomatoes, which abound in the Italy of today, were only introduced after the discovery of South America by Christopher Columbus in 1492. Coffee came from Arabia. For the more affluent in the peninsula meat and fish and a large variety of game including peacocks, song birds and wild boar figured largely on their tables. These were frequently served with rich sauces and spices. Sugar was scarce, so expensive, and often replaced by honey. For the rich no meal was complete without a *"torta."* For them meals on high days and holidays were gargantuan to be seen in the description of wedding feasts.

Dress codes in England were delineated by what were known as "the sumptuary laws". The word derives from the Latin adjective *sumptuari* meaning pertaining to or regulating expense. Correspondingly the English word sumptuous implies magnificence. Carters, ploughmen and herdsmen were forbidden the use of cloth and restricted to blanket homespun wool costing 12d or less. Yeoman and tradesmen were forbidden the use of silk, embroidery, buttons, decorative daggers, rings, jewels and collars or chains made of gold or silver. The average man was simply dressed in homespun wool. Peasant women were only allowed to wear veils made of yarn, and no furs except rabbit, cat or fox. English women of the time tended to wear buttoned doublets over their dresses

In northern Italy cloth was more readily available than in

England but dyeing was very expensive. As in England only the very rich were able to wear the colourful robes depicted in paintings of the time. The dress code was governed by even stricter sumptuary laws than those at home. In 1272 there were already fifty-four named regulations which rose to eighty-three in the 14th century. Hats, their shape and colour, played a prominent part in the dress code and portrayed the status and power of the family of the wearer. Unmarried young ladies must go bareheaded and wear their hair loose, a prerogative also shared by queens.

Colours also played a significant part in dress codes. Yellow for example was reserved for Jews. Long tunics were the order of the day. In Romagna the length of tunic was restricted to *un palmo di terra,* one hand's length from the floor. The fashion for shorter robes crept in from France. This culture was initially greeted with disapproval in the same way that mini-skirts were first received in England in the 1960s. The luxurious fabrics traded from the east were confined to the upper classes and were too expensive for the average man and woman. By the time of Hawkwood's arrival the long tunics worn by the upper classes had been replaced in the1340s by more revealing figure hugging dresses for the ladies and elaborately inflated knee length trousers under tight jerkins for the men. Often the new dresses of the ladies would be enhanced by a bejewelled girdle dropped across their hips. They frequently had wide sleeved tops and trains, depending on their status. Many of these new fashions were influenced by the French styles at the Papal court of Avignon.

In the field of the visual arts the peninsula was greatly more sophisticated and advanced than England of the day. Outside the precincts of great cathedrals or churches, whose walls were largely decorated with frescoes and sculptures, few individual artists or paintings existed in England. There were monastic libraries where the art of illuminating manuscripts throve, but in secular England of the time the visual arts were limited. In this new country over the alps the English would have been exposed to the dazzling gold ground panels of the great late 13th and early 14th century Sienese Masters who flourished in the city's golden age when she ruled most of southern Tuscany. Unlike in England, paintings adorned municipal as well as religious buildings.

The authors of these works, led by the painter Duccio di Buoninsegna [1278–1318], numbered amongst them the painters:; Cimabue[1240–60] ; Bernardo Daddi [1290–1348]; the Lorenzetti brothers, one of whom Ambrogio [1285–1348], executed the famous fresco series representing the Good and Bad Government in Siena's town hall; Simone Martini[1285–1344] and his assistant Lippo Memmi [1290–c1347] and the great Florentine artist and architect Giotto [1267–1337], discovered as a shepherd boy by Cimabue. Giotto became famous for departing from the stylised Byzantine style by introducing a form of perspective and human expression into pictorial images.In the field of sculpture the way was led by Nicolo Pisano and his son, Giovanni, who designed the façade of Siena cathedral.

Many of the lives of these artists were cut short by the

plague adding to the decrease in population throughout the northern states. Then in 1355 Siena was overthrown by the ghibelline supporters of Emperor Charles 1V which led to its political demise. With this, artistic activity further declined through lack of patronage.

Among the few painters who survived the plague and who were active in Florence at the time of Hawkwood's arrival was Orcagna [1308-68]. who had been commissioned to create a tabernacle in the church of Orsanmichele. This chuch was built on the site of a small oratory whose upper floor had previously served as the city's granary. Andrea da Firenze[fl1343-1377] would have been working on the frescoes in Spanish Chapel in Santa Maria Novella. Niccolo di Pietro Gerini [fl.1368-1415] was another of the few painters who continued working in Florence the duration of Hawkwood's life in the peninsula, whose work formed a link between the stylistic innovations of Giotto and Fra Angelico [b. c. 1395].

In Arezzo, where Hawkwood fought several times, the works we see to-day by Spinello Aretino were probably yet to be executed as he was not born till 1372. The city already would have boasted several works of Margarito di Arezzo who flourished in the middle of the 13th century. Here the cathedral, whose construction commenced at the end of the 13th century, would have existed in some form. The 12th century church of Santa Maria della Pieve, with its colonnaded façade and polyptych by Pietro Lorenzetti, would have already been well established and is unchanged to the present day. Hawkwood might have worshipped in the church of San Domenico, with its impressive crucifix by Cimabue. The Basilica of San Francesco would have existed, but the famous Legend of the Cross by Piero della Francesca was a hundred years away.

Many great masters of the future were born whilst Hawkwood was in the peninsula, whose work he mostly never saw. These were to achieve fame in the 15th century, paving the way for what is now called the Renaissance with its revival of interest in antiquity and its intensification of enquiry into the physical world. Paolo Uccello author of the posthumous memorial to Hawkwood never met his subject, who died a good five years before he was born and yet, there he unwittingly portrays this English mercenary stepping on to the threshold of the Renaissance.

With regard to religion, the English soldiers of the 14th century shared the same Christian Faith with the people of the peninsula, so the services and forms of worship would have been familiar. The churches with their rich marble interiors illumined by gold ground paintings would have been somewhat different to the grey Saxon, Norman and Gothic churches of England, whose austere interior stone walls were decorated covered with frescoes.

In the political and military scene England was far superior to the peninsula. The country was more or less united under one very strong monarch Edward III whose army was famous for its discipline and strength. Being a collection of princely states the peninsula did not have an army as such. Although conscription existed there was no regular training and many princes preferred to secure the help of foreign mercenaries. The English soldiers were far hardier than their indigenous peers – perhaps because they came from northern climes. They were happy to attack under cover of night and fully prepared to operate in harsh winter weather, a custom alien to the Italians! These characteristics pertain to this day.

The impact Hawkwood and his colleagues on the Italians must have been daunting. The military turnout of the English was impeccable. They took great pride in their uniforms which were immaculate. With the aid of the marrow of smoked goats legs they burnished their armour till it glittered. Their shining breast plates and white flags earned them the soubriquet of the White Company. The English troops must have instilled a certain amount of fear, and probably envy, in their enemies by their bravery, ruthlessness and unorthodox military behaviour. One can understand why the rather cowardly Italians nicknamed them "devils incarnate". However they also instilled respect in their opponents on account of their efficiency, team spirit and discipline. These qualities, largely non-existent amongst the Italians, gave them huge advantages.

Above all else the English enjoyed superior military skills and weaponry. For instance, the Italians had never abandoned the clumsy short ranged crossbow in warfare. The English, who were renowned for their archery, utilised the longbow with its range of 400 metres. It was referred to in contemporary Italian writing as an *archone* We read that: '*they carry bows on their backs* ....

the foot-soldiers have big and powerful bows that reach from their heads to the ground and being drawn, shoot great long arrows.'

At a time when warfare was largely conducted on horseback, the English adopted a tactic whereby, before reaching the enemy lines, they dismounted from their chargers which they left in safety with a page. Each knight then advanced with a squire jointly bearing the heavy lance in a horizontal position to form a human grid at eye level. As the mounted enemy troops charged towards their adversaries the horses fell prey to this grid of pikes, speedily dislodging their knights who were left at the mercy of the aggressor. From this military tactic derives the expression "freelance". This exercise must have proved most unnerving to the local companies of cavalry to whom such a practice, although originally adopted by the Romans had long since been forgotten.

Pisan assignment

The city of Pisa, where Hawkwood found himself in 1363, had been an important commercial port and naval base since Roman times. The city was an ally of Milan whose allegiance was to the Holy Roman Emperor leader of the Ghibelline faction. As such it was opposed to Genoa on the seas and Lucca and Florence on the land, all of whom adhered to the Guelphic faction.

The city had enjoyed its heyday in the 12th and early13th centuries. As its harbour gradually began to silt up and it became wracked by internal political strife and disease, its maritime empire floundered, its wealth diminished, and its pre-eminence ceded to its rival Genoa. The legacy of its maritime and financial demise is the thankful survival of the city's romanesque architecture and sculpture. Through lack of funds, her buildings were largely left untouched by the subsequent renaissance and baroque style of later years. Hawkwood would have been familiar with the Campo dei Miracoli as we see it today. He would have been able to admire the cathedral, designed by the Greek architect Buschetto. He and his men would have been confronted with, and probably both bewildered and astounded by the work of those two great sculptors – Nicolo and Giovanni Pisano – father and son – on the marble pulpits in the cathedral and baptistery. This latter building would have been standing, with the exception of its dome, which was added at the end of the 14th century. The bell tower would have been almost complete. Unfortunately the German architect, Guglielmo, did not secure the piles sufficiently and, according to the 16th century art historian, Giorgio Vasari, the tower already showed signs of sinking before it had attained half its height.

Even in her weakened political state Pisa's position on the Mediterranean at the mouth of the River Arno remained srategic. At the time of Hawkwood's arrival in 1364 she was still a ripe target for both Milan and Florence, neither of which cities had alternative outlets to the sea for their trade. Sensing this threat and without adequate internal military support Pisa was only too anxious to engage these newly arrived English soldiers .

Having signed up the English raiders, under the leadership of the German mercenary Sterz, for the princely sum of forty thousand florins, Pisa's first assignment to them was to humble Florence, and to reduce as far as possible her military potential. It was not for nothing that Pisa's heraldic beast was a fox and that of its rival, Florence, a lion. In June 1363 Sterz led the White Company, reinforced by Pisan troops, towards the city. Naturally Florence had got wind of the attack and had withdrawn all her men into the confines of the city. Sterz was no great strategist and, apart from harassing and provoking the citizens with showers of poisoned arrows and other ammunition over the walls, seemed to have no serious plan for attack. Hawkwood meanwhile realised the necessity of establishing a nearby base from where to attack Florence. He decided on Figline, a fortified village situated thirty miles south of the city, overlooking the fertile plain of Val d'Arno with its plentiful supply of grain. Figline fell to him with little opposition, due possibly to the connivance of its pro-Pisan factions.

Devastated and humiliated by the capture of their local stronghold and the prospect of facing a winter short of grain, Florence sent out her army to confront the mercenary force at Incisa which lay on a bend of the river Arno about four miles north of Figline. Her Captain General, Ranuncio Farnese, made the strategic mistake of spreading his forces too widely enabling the invaders an easy victory and the capture of Incisa. This battle took place on October 13th 1363, the feast of the royal english saint, King Edward the Confessor.

By December Hawkwood had replaced Sterz as commander of the White Company. His obvious superiority in the Florentine engagement must have earned him the respect of both his men and his masters. In January 1364, after the death of the previous incumbent, Messer Chizelli, Pisa elected him their Captain General. For this privilege Hawkwood demanded a fee of 150,000 florins for six months to which the city reluctantly agreed.

In early February, 1364 Hawkwood led out once again an Anglo-Pisan contingent to Florence. How often does today's traveller, as speeds down the superstrada in his motor car from Pisa to Florence occasionally admiring an ancient fort perched on a hill over the river Arno, ever give a thought to the difficulties in making the same journey with an army in the year 1364? The obvious route was down the bank of the river which links the two

49

cities,but with horses and all their equipment competing with the sinking muddy riverbed, Hawkwood chose an alternative route. With a collective force of five thousand he opted to proceed through the plain of Pistoia, and to approach Florence from the north via Prato.   Aware of the reluctance of the indigenous armies to fight in the winter, he foresaw little opposition. However he had not reckoned with the ferocity of the men of Pistoia. Believed to be descended from the Roman conspirator Cataline, it was not for nothing that Dante described the city as *a den of noxious beasts*. The city was renowned for its ironwork and was particularly known for the production of a type of gun named after the city *pistole* what we today call a pistol. In the event the White Company suffered such severe losses at the hands of the Pistoians that they were forced to withdraw back to Pisa with their tails between their legs.

It was not until the end of April when Hawkwood rebuilt his company with the enlistment of three thousand German mercenaries that he managed to seize and occupy the town of Fiesole in the hills above Florence. Once arrived in the neighbourhood, for the virile young English troops together with their brother German soldiers in arms, the harassment of Florence and her outlying territories was a sport to be enjoyed. Having taunted and pillaged the enemy all day they made merry all night with dancing, jousts and feasts in the local village squares ,no doubt also enjoying the local damsels and wines.

Legend tells us that Hawkwood himself lodged in the villa of Poggio Gherardo. Today a convent, the villa commands a strategic view over the city of Florence and the Arno valley below. which would have been a most appropriate foothold for a military commander. From this hilltop 14th century Florence would have resembled a forest of lookout towers surrounded by high secure walls. These lookout towers, originally designed for defence, and universally used by all low lying cities in the peninsula during medieval times, gradually became status symbols, which led to competition amongst cities and the families therein as to whom could build the highest. Eventually a law was passed restricting their dimensions. In most cities today the towers have been lowered or smothered by subsequent buildings and are often no longer clearly visible. The well known exception is the town of San Gimigniano.

Florence in 1364, as yet untouched by the Renaissance, presented a very different picture to the city with which we are familiar to-day. The architecture at the time extant was largely the work of Arnolfo di Cambio, born in 1232, the son of a German architect Maestro Jacopo known as Lapo. On his father's death he was considered the best architect in Tuscany. He built the walls of Florence in 1284. He continued to design many churches and convents culminating with the cathedral for which he made a model directing that: "*the walls should be encrusted with marbles, cornices, pilasters, carved foliage, figures and other ornaments*". The cornerstone was laid in 1298 and the building completed by 1360. The cathedral was called Santa Reparata. The Bargello, or prison, was built though not yet enlarged. The Baptistery was already in situ. Giotto's Campanile was upstanding. Orsanmichele,used as as a grain market in 13th century, was re-converted into a church after the appearance of the miraculous image of the Virgin Mary in the middle of the 14th century, and adopted by the many guilds of the city. The Ponte Vecchio would have spanned the river Arno. The churches of Santa Croce, Santa Maria Novella were in existence. The Piazza della Signoria and its palazzo, now known as the Palazzo Vecchio, with its great halls and tower were there, but no fountains, no Loggia and no Uffizi Gallery. The Palazzi Strozzi or Pitti were yet to come.

The battle day was set for May 1st, a public holiday usually celebrated with merry-making and auguries of love, when it was hoped the minds of the Florentines would be far removed from warfaring! Hawkwood and his company set out across the River Arno and occupied the hills of Arcetri and Bellosguardo, rendering havoc to the neighbouring countryside. No farm or orchard was left unharmed. The city of Florence, however, proved too hard a nut to crack. One possible reason why Hawkwood's assault failed was that, although his solders were adept at scaling walls, they did not possess sophisticated enough siege equipment so stood no chance of storming fortresses or capturing strongly defended walled cities.

Florence, although it had escaped occupation by the aggressor, could not tolerate seeing all its outlying territories, on which it relied for provisions, overtaken by its enemies. Unofficially it took the opportunity to bribe onto its side many of the aggrieved members of the White Company, chiefly Germans, who felt deprived of their plunder and were only too happy to defect to the victor. Hawkwood, unlike his foreign peers, always proved himself to be in this, and every subsequent instance, a man of his word. Fidelity was the keynote of his character, so having made a *condotta* with Pisa he remained loyal to that city. He therefore led the desultory 800 men remaining from his company of 2000 back to Pisa to face the consequences. In the circumstances these did not prove to be too dire. It is probable that Pisa knew the dice were weighted too heavily against them to succeed in their assault of Florence and, after all, Hawkwood had managed to inspire a certain amount of fear into the enemy ranks and wreck a fair amount of damage in their neighbouring lands.

In July the Florentines, under Galeotto Malatesta, decided to capitalise on their swollen ranks by challenging and badly defeating the diminished Pisan army at Cascina. They burnt the town of Livorno forcing Hawkwood to retreat to San Savino. 2000 prisoners were taken. To add insult to injury, but to our subsequent advantage, these prisoners were put to work by their captors to construct the beautiful Loggia dei Pisani in Florence, which stands to this day on the side of the Duomo. This proved the final straw for the domoralised Pisans troops and it was not long before revolution broke out in their city.

Out of this political confusion came forward an ambitious and wealthy merchant who craftily usurped the position of doge by negotiating a loan from the Visconti on the undertaking that

Pisa and Lucca would remain satellites of Milan, as long as he was in power. This Giovanni Agnello was an unlovable arrogant little dictator. He won over the city elders, known as the *Anziani*, by declaring that the Blessed Virgin had revealed to him in a dream that he must assume the dogeship of Pisa for one year, and subsequently for life. He at first endeared himself to the population with the knowledge that he could guarantee payment to the soldiers, but it was not long before they were disillusioned. However, with Hawkwood's help, Agnello was duly re-elected. The extent of the doge's gratitude and affection for Hawkwood is marked by his naming in baptism his second son *Francesco Aguto*, which is the variation most used by the Italians of Hawkwood's, to them, unpronounceable name. Acuto meaning sharp also doubled up as an appropriate nickname for this English raider, who became known as *Giovanni Acuto*.

Late in 1364 Agnello concluded a peace with Florence at the costly price of 10,000 florins a year for ten years. To put this sum in perspective ten florins was the annual pay of a maid. Agnello came to an untimely and infra dig end a year or two later at Lucca when breaking his thigh by falling through a collapsed overcrowded, specially erected, portico in the cloisters where he was delivering a welcoming speech to the Emperor Charles IV.

The vipers of Milan

The truce with Florence was good news for Pisa, but bad news for Hawkwood as it left him without employment. However by 1365 he had managed to rebuild the White Company and fortunately his services were soon enlisted by Pisa's powerful Ghibelline ally Bernabo Visconti, Lord of Milan, enemy of both Florence and the Church. On behalf of his new master he set out to harrass papal lands but was given a sound wigging by the German papal troops and suffered a severe defeat at Perugia.

Having lost large numbers of his own men he joined up with one of Bernabo's natural sons, Ambrogio Visconti, and his company of San Giorgio. Allied to Ambrogio were a group of Germans, under Baumgarten and Count John of Hapsburg, forming a truly international league. Ambrogio took his section off to the Kingdom of Naples where he was defeated and imprisoned by the mad Queen Joanna. The remainder of the band joined Hawkwood in ravaging the lands between Siena and Perugia culminating in routing the Sienese at Montalcinello and defeating both them and the Perugians at the battle of Ponte San Giovanni doing untold harm to the countryside as they went. The Sienese made countless overtures to the company of San Giorgio to spare them and theirs, but it was only with a bribe of six thousand florins that they finally managed to succeed. To raise this sum Siena, whose coffers were bare and who was very much a

city in decline, had to take a loan from her wine duties.
Florence for her part won five years reprieve of attack in exchange
for the sum of 10,500 florins and permission for the company`s
troops to pass over her lands once a year as long as they inflicted
no harm on the way.

One of the incidents of the many battles with papal forces
to which we have a living testament was the seizure and
plundering of the monastery of San Galgano lying between Siena
and Massa Marittima. This was the most important religious
complex on Sienese territory at the time. It was a cistercian
foundation whose patron San Galgano attracted monks from
much hated France and the noble families of Siena. As such it was
a prime target for the ghibelline Company of San Giorgio. Their
aim, in true mercenary fashion, was not to raise the abbey to the
ground but to remove the leaden tiles from the roof and plunder
their treasures, which they duly did. The high value of lead was
an attractive and useful booty for a mercenary.

An element of chicanery is suggested by evidence of some
speculation that the Sienese authorities made an agreement with
the condottieri on the division of the proceeds! The walls of what
became known as the Abbey of the Open Sky remain standing to
this day.

Another incident further north which enhanced
Hawkwood's reputation was his brilliant defence of Borgoforte,
a recently established Milanese fortification on the river Po,
against the forces of the German Emperor Charles IV.

The Imperialists had planned to break the embankments of the river above the fort. Hawkwood with a fraction of the numbers of his opponents, under cover of night, breached the downstream embankments thus flooding the plain and entrenching the enemy in their tracks. This is but one example of his outstanding expertise in military strategy.

A measure of the reputation that Hawkwood was acquiring, as a force to be reckoned with, is illustrated by a legend in 1367. When Pope Urban V, the successor to Innocent VI and another much hated Frenchman, decided to try and return to Rome, His Holiness set sail from Avignon in a Venetian galley proposing to call in at Livorno on the way. However on spotting that the greeting party, headed by Doge Agnello of Pisa, was accompanied by Hawkwood, the pope was too frightened to disembark so continued on his way without disembarking.

His Holiness was probably wise to be suspicious. Edward III was already at loggerheads with the papacy over her greedy levies of taxes from his subjects which amounted to five times those levied by the monarchy. It was said that the Pope's revenue from England alone was larger than that of any prince in Christendom. Morevover Urban well knew that Edward supported the mercenaries and was also allied with his present enemy, the Visconti of Milan. He was wise therefore to be suspicious of Hawkwood`s presence which may well even have been at Edward`s command.

As it turned out, although Urban was triumphantly

received in Rome, the task of bringing order to the Roman government, and discipline to the clergy proved too difficult. Despite the urgings of the visionary, St Bridget of Sweden, for him to remain in Rome and her gloomy prophecy of his death should he return, after three years the frightened and discouraged Urban made tracks back to Avignon. Alas the prophecy was punctually fulfilled. Three months after his arrival in the French city the pope died; dressed in a monk's habit he was laid out on an austere mat. It was not until six years later in 1376 that Urban's successor Gregory XI achieved the return of the papacy to Rome.

A royal wedding

1368 found Hawkwood in Milan on completely different business from his usual military pursuits. Here we find him for the first time in a role which he was asked to play on many subsequent occasions by his king, with whom he remained in close touch throughout his career. Edward III had contracted the marriage of his recently widowed third son, Lionel, Duke of Clarence with Violante, the 13 year old daughter of Galeazzo Visconti. For the Visconti, ever socially mobile, to be allied to the throne of England was yet another feather in their cap. Galeazzo's son Giangaleazzo, of whom we will hear later, was already married to Isabelle de Valois, daughter of the king of France which had cost the Visconti 200,000 ducats, the equivalent of the ransom demanded by the English king who had previously taken him hostage!   For Edward, ever impecunious and reliant on loans from Italy, the marriage of Violante was of great political and economic advantage as the bride's dowry was 200,000 florins.

Clarence set out with his suite from England attended by 400 men–at–arms. As he passed through France he was entertained lavishly by the French court and nobility. The feasting, jousting and, no doubt wenching, far exceeded even any modern day stag party. Once arrived in Lombardy Edward put his son under the protection of his loyal knight Sir John Hawkwood whom we find recorded as "Captain of the Duke's Guard", along with Lord Edward de Spencer as "Steward".

A contemporary account describes the greeting party who went to receive the English prince at the gates of Milan:

'80 bridesmaids dressed in scarlet gowns with white sleeves embroidered with trefoils attached to golden girdles; the knights in shining armour and the horses draped with white or purple brocade.'

They must have made a colourful and ostentatious cortège. The local writer sadly fails to give us a description of the English retinue. Was this out of chauvinistic reasons or were the visitors too drab, overhung and travel stained in appearance to be worth noting?

The marriage itself was a magnificent affair in which the Visconti had spared no expense to impress the English, and the world in general, with their power and wealth. The guest list was international including the great and the good from diverse circles. Amongst the more cultured guests Petrarch, dressed, as his wont, in shepherds clothes, must have stood out by the simplicity of his attire. Froissart would almost certainly been there, but no evidence exists to substantiate the legend of the English poet Geoffrey Chaucer's presence, although in his role as former page in the household of the Duke of Clarence who became one of his earliest patrons, it is a plausible story. There does exist a warrant from the royal privy seal, dated 17th July 1368 for a licence for *nostre ame vallet* Geffrey Chaucer to pass at Dover across the sea, which could corroborate the story. Maddeningly it is a month too late as the marriage is documented as taking place in June. Chaucer began his life as an attendant in royal circles where he had the opportunity to learn Latin and study courtly life. The poet did make three recorded visits to Italy on missions for the Crown where he gained valuable material for his writings. Even without his presence at the wedding it is interesting to visualise these learned writers and poets mingling with the warriors and crowned heads of Europe. In what tongue, for instance, would they conversed? The educated classes in England at the time still spoke chiefly French, although Edward III in 1362 had replaced it with english as the official language. Hawkwood, it is known, learnt italian at an early stage after his arrival. Would he perhaps acted as interpreter for his compatriots?

The wedding banquet we are told ran to 30 courses all accompanied by presentations of gifts of both animate and inanimate objects, as no doubt was usual at the time. We have descriptions of the first three courses:

At the call of the trumpet arrived the first course of meat and fish; two gilded suckling pigs from whose mouths exuded billowing flames; gilded hares and pikes, a large calf, roast trout, quails and partridges. The accompanying gifts included twelve pairs of greyhounds with silken collars secured with gilded buckles; twelve pairs of bloodhounds, twelve hawks, their collars with brass bells, their troos and hoods of silk with silver studs; twelve pairs of hunstman linked by chains; six goshawks secured with enamelled silver chains. The second course consisted of roast duck, herons, carp, pork, fat capons in garlic sauce, capons and meat in lemon sauce, fish in sauce, pasties of ox meat and fat eels. The accompanying gifts included: Six falcons with velvet caps encrusted with pearls, steel buckles and silver muzzles; 12 sets of armour for jousting and 12 sets for combat; and two saddles with silver mounts. The third course was of meat, fish, galantine of roast kid, hare, goat, brains, capons and pullets in red and green sauce, peahens with cabbage and French beans, salted tongue, rabbits, roast peacock and duck, junket, cheese and marzipan. The accompanying gifts included twelve pieces of gold brocade and twelve of silk, six silver basins, gilded and enamelled; silver flasks full of malmsey and vernaccia, lances, helmets, six large steeds, six green velvet cloaks with red buttons and tassels and silk pendants; six red velvet mantels with gold tassels, a heavy coat applied with pearls, a large gold flower, a silver basin with rubies, diamonds and pearls. All these dishes were served on ornate silver gilt and jewel encrusted platters and the wines contained in ornately decorated flagons.

The marriage festivities would also have included dancing, jousting and all manner of merrymaking till the early hours of the morning. Galeazzo, the father of the bride, retired early to his chamber to dream up new monuments, and Bernabo, her warrior uncle, immediately parted for battle.

The bridegroom did not enjoy his wife, or her fortune, for long. Within three months of the marriage he died from mysterious causes. Poison was one of the most common ways of doing away with people in high places at the time and foul play of this nature was of course suspected. It is not impossible to imagine that the English stomach of the bridegroom had succumbed to a surfeit of the French and Italian culinary delights with which he had been plied ever since he left his native land. Meanwhile the thirteen year old bride, for whom the marriage with this elderly English Prince must have been in any case somewhat of an ordeal, cannot have suffered undue grief.

For a month or two Despencer and Hawkwood sought vengeance on the suspected murderer of their master. One of the suspects of Clarence's demise was Bernabo himself but he was proved innocent and Hawkwood returned to his service.

Arms and the man

One of Hawkwood's most colourful adventures was later in 1368.
Feigning to be an independent agent sacked by the Visconti, he
set off to aid the Perugians who had obtained an alliance with his
masters, in an attack against the Papal troops at Arezzo. This ruse
however did not work and he was heavily defeated by the
Guelphs at Porta Buia and allegedly imprisoned in Arezzo.
Although there is no concrete evidence to this effect the fact that
there are no records of Hawkwood's activities for a year suggests
the story may be true.

When next we hear of him in 1369 he had managed to
extricate himself from prison, possibly ransomed by his friends in
Pisa. Once free he immediately began reconstructing his
company. Having mustered his troops Hawkwood, with
Visconti's blessing, rode into the papal states once more to the aid
of those Perugians who had rebelled against His Holiness. Urban,
who had refused to land at Livorno two years previously, was
blockaded in nearby Montefiascone and fled to Viterbo. Urban
tried to bribe the enemy troops to join his side with promises of
indulgences, but to no effect. Hawkwood and his followers
preferred to remain with Visconti.

Throughout his career in Italy Hawkwood's fealty

belonged unswervingly to his own English sovereign. An illustration of this loyalty is how Hawkwood's was the onlycavalry company, allegedly, who refused to take an oath of fealty to the Patriarch of Aquitaine in his capacity as vicar of the emperor Charles IV. The Patriarch had to content himself with a promise of their obedience.

In the summer of 1369 Hawkwood got his own back on the Florentines by delivering them a resounding defeat at the battle of Cascina thus reversing the tables on their previous victory on the same ground in 1364.

Later that year Visconti despatched Hawkwood to San Miniato the, erstwhile tuscan seat of the Holy Roman Emperor, now a Florentine stronghold strategically placed between Florence and Pisa. The Florentines flattered themselves they would have no difficulty with their superior numbers in defending themselves. However they had not taken into sufficient account the wiles of their adversary. The tactics he employed on this occasion were to simulate a false retreat which fooled the enemy into thinking their invaders were on the move. These tactics he carried out in the following way.

Realising his numeric disadvantage, Hawkwood uses one of his favourite tricks. He makes a great show of fording the river Arno with a portion of his younger men as if they were retreating. The Florentine cavalry chases after them along the river bed only to find their horses hooves sink and stick into the soft mud, hampering their progress and forming a sitting target for the remainder of the English troops, whom Hawkwood has cunningly placed in ambush on either side of the river. For the Florentines this was an ignominious defeat. For the Visconti, despite the great victory Hawkwood had obtained on their behalf, no conclusive results were achieved . They continued to plunder and sack the surrounding countryside to no political advantage. They were forced to conclude a treaty with the Florentines in november that year.

Hawkwood remained at large fighting interalia the Pisans and the papal states. One might wonder at this point whether Hawkwood had an urge to return to his native land. However the political situation at home was to say the least unsettled. Ever since the peace of Brétigny Edward III had begun to lose the plot. The extensive loss of life and resulting hardships from the plague, together with the imposition of increasing taxes to cover Edward's international loans, were two of the main causes of unrest amongst his people. The military successes which had flushed England with pride had passed into a long series of disasters to which no-one was anxious to subscribe.

Moreover the seeming triumph of the treaty of Brétigny had in real terms damaged Edward's cause in the South of France. By the cessation of Aquitaine to the king in full sovereignty, perversely the traditional claim on which his strength lay lost its force. Whereas the Gascons had clung to their former duke, albeit a foreigner, and treasured their independent province, now they resisted their incorporation with northern France.
England had less appeal.

A deal with the Pope

In 1372 Hawkwood achieved another major victory by defeating
and capturing, at the castle of Rubiera, the Captain of a company
which outnumbered his by two to one who was coming to the
aid of Hawkwood's old boss, the Marquis of Monferrat, at war
with Galeazzo Visconti. He then suddenly threw in his contract
with the Milanese and joined the service of the pope,
by now Gregory XI. There is no obvious explanation of this
precipitous action. Too slow payment of wages was the outward
cause for the break. Maybe the refusal of Bianca, Galeazzo
Visconti's wife, to allow their young son to join the fry had
something to do with his decision. True, the papacy had been
wooing him for some time. Perhaps even Hawkwood was
becoming frustrated by the tyranny of the Visconti.
Perhaps he just needed a change.

Having put himself under the command of the Papal
Legate at Bologna inMay 1373 he found himself opposing the
Milanese at the battle of Panaro and defeating Galeazzo Visconti,
his erstwhile ally and patron, on the river Chiese. Such was the
amorality of a mercenary. Hawkwood may also have wanted to
show Milan what a good man they had lost in him! His
honeymoon with the papacy was of short duration. Although
Pope Gregory peppered him with letters calling Hawkwood
dilecto filio [dear son], urging him to fight Bernabo with all his

might and telling him to be patient for his fees, no money was forthcoming. Even when Hawkwood sent his fellow countryman, John Brise of Essex, to treat with Gregory no firm answer was given. During Hawkwood's command of Bologna the Papal Legate banned the export of corn from the Romagna and also closed the appenine passes, to which the Florentines took exception, allying themselves with their former enermies, the Milanese. Taking advantage of Hawkwood's temporary absence the Florentines liberated Bologna and the English feared to return.

After two years in 1374, without the wherewithall to pay his troops, Hawkwood parted company with the Church and set out on his own.

Florence beckons

Now his own boss, owing allegiance to no–one, and having to find the wherewithal with which to pay his hungry troops Hawkwood posed a serious threat to all parties and states in the north of the peninsula who feared coming under his attack. A measure of their alarm is voiced by that inveterate correspondent Catherine Becincasa, the future St. Catherine of Siena, who was moved to dictate one of her many letters urging Hawkwood to leave tuscany in peace . She begins by reminding him that he had already engaged himself to go to the Holy Land to join the Crusades. Although there is no evidence of Hawkwood's

commitment this possibly might have been true in 1365. The
lady continues: *therefore I pray you sweetly for the sake of Jesus
Christ for since God and our Holy Father have ordained for us to
go against the Infidel to no longer war against the Christians.
because it is an offence to God, but go to oppose them [the Turks]
for it is a great cruelty that we who are Christians should persecute
one another,...so that you from being a servant of the devil,
might become a manly and true knight.* Although the crusades
themselves were over, it was still regarded the duty of every
Christian knight to "go on Crusade"and moreover Catherine was
keen to promote another.

      Catherine Becincase, the youngest of twenty or more
children of a Sienese dyer, dedicated her life to prayer and
penance from an early age, becoming a Dominican tertiary. Only
after years of solitude did she begin mingling in society.
This she did first through nursing the sick and subsequently
enlarging her circle to groups of followers in the Catholic faith,
who travelled with her around Italy preaching repentance and
reform. Catherine liked to express her ideals in dialogue and
letters, all of which she dictated as she never learned to write, but
for which she became famous! Although very surprising to us,
this was not so unusual in 14th century Italy where learning was
largely confined to men, and chiefly to clerics.

      In her later years Catherine became very involved with the
affairs of both State and Church. Her influence, it was popularly
but erroneously believed, had been decisive in bringing about the
final return of the papacy to Rome from Avignon in 1377.

She herself would have been delighted to be given the credit for this event towards which she certainly did lend all her endeavours even to the extent of following by road in the footsteps of Gregory XI's return journey by sea. Catherine was a modern day Christian fanatic. After her death in 1380 she became Siena`s patron and a figure of international importance. Eighty years later, in 1460 she was canonised, largely through the influence of her champion and later biographer, Raymond de Capua, Master General of the Dominican order. It is interesting that it was only as recently as 1970 was she declared a Doctor of the Church.

To return to her letter to Hawkwood, he declined the great lady's exhortation. The Pope's representative simultaneously was requesting him to fight fellow Christians and erstwhile employers nearer to home. He turned his immediate attention to the oppression of the tuscan cities as Catherine had feared. Already stricken by famine after a bad harvest and the ban of import of wheat from Romagna imposed by the French cardinal, they proved only too ready to buy him off. Pisa offered him a fee of 30,000 florins for which he agreed "not to burn, make prisoners or slaves of Pisans and not to enter the town with any weapons except a sword and knife" Arezzo, whom he attacked, paid him 8,500 florins to withdraw. Siena was also invited to subscribe.

However it was from Florence with its burgeoning commerce where Hawkwood saw his main chance of extracting money. The Republic was still allied with the Church who emerge as playing a very duplicitous role in their political liaisons. Late in 1375 finally exposed to their treachery Florence broke the

Guelphic Agreement whereby she was allied with the pope against the feuding ghibelline aristocracy, who were in their turn allied with the Holy Roman Emperor.

Now Hawkwood found himself courted by both the Papacy and the Republic. Perhaps, persuaded that he had drained Tuscany dry, he decided to play off one against the other. Knowing full well the pope's disinclination to pay for his services it was perhaps the gift of the villa Montisfertini which Gregory offered him in lieu of back wages that finally tipped the scales.

It was a very byzantine arrangement as simultaneously, and egged on by the Pope, Hawkwood continued dialogue with Florence. He demanded from her a fee of 130,000 florins which he knew she was unable to pay. Florence was apalled by this demand. However, terrified of the threat of Hawkwood's troops descending on the city, it sent back the Ambassadors with instructions to make agreement at any price. The Cardinal Legate surreptitiously intervened and offered Florence a contribution of half this sum in lieu of back wages to Hawkwood. In this duplicitous way a deal was concluded by which Hawkwood agreed to fight for the Pope but to refrain from attacking Florence or any of her territories for five years. This was the beginning of an affiliation with Florence which would last in various forms for the rest of his life. Hawkwood also managed to extract from the Signoria of the Republic the assurance of an annual pension should he leave Italy, which leads one to speculate that his long term aim was to return home to his much loved king and country.

For the next two years Hawkwood remained ostensibly

employed by the pope, but was simultaneously under an obligation to keep his agreement with Florence. The city did not have need of him for the moment as she was very much engaged in her own internal dispute, in which she was not anxious to involve Hawkwood, unless being victorious he might wish to seize power over her. They need not have feared. Hawkwood's politics were confined to the interests of his own sovereign and not the internal feuds of Italian city States.

The Church at war

One of Florence's concerns was that Pope Gregory XI, might turn his anger against them for non payment of debts incurred in the wars against the Visconti, and move all his disgruntled unpaid troops on to Florentine soil. In order to counteract this threat Florence decided to organise a general insurrection against the Church, inflaming the general discontent of the people against the ecclesiastical administrators. This was a relatively easy exercise as the Italian populace heartily disliked being governed by French clerics. The insurrection started in Viterbo, north of Rome, and spread rapidly to neighbouring Umbria.

On hearing the news the bolognese Papal Legate secretly commissioned Hawkwood to go to the aid of the much disliked

Abbot of Perugia, another Frenchman, Gerard du Puys, who was
mustering all the troops he could to go to the rescue of his
neighbouring ecclesiastical colleagues. Hawkwood pretended to
be working as a freelance agent,thus hoping not to be seen as
taking sides. The whole expedition went horribly wrong. No
sooner had Hawkwood and his troops departed from Perugia the
citizens rose up against the diabolical abbot and forced him to take
refuge with his guard in the castle of Montmaggiore.
Considering the numerous atrocities the abbot had committed
against the Perugians one has every sympathy with their action
which was not purely racist in motive. To make matters worse
Hawkwood also failed in his mission to neighbouring Citta di
Castello. Here the ecclesiastics had shut themselves up in their
citadel and were forced to surrender to the townsfolk. The
whole affair was a disaster for the Church who, within a period of
ten days, lost eighty strongholds. Although the Abbot of
Montmaggiore and his followers managed to hold out until the
end of the year, they finally were forced to abandon the city and
were taken by Hawkwood under armed guard to the Romagna.

In spite of the fact that Hawkwood had not been
successful on behalf of the Church he had still gone to a great deal
of trouble and expense in their service for which his employers, as
usual, seemed reluctant to recompense him. Eventually, in the
spring of 1376, Pope Gregory decided to reward him with
property in lieu of fees. He gave Hawkwood the lordships of
Bagnocavallo, Conselice and Cotignola in the Romagna on the
fluvial plain between Ravenna and Bologna. The Pope, no

doubt. had his reasons for choosing the location of this gift as Romagna was a troublesome area in which he needed support. Of these properties Hawkwood chose to make his headquarters at the most substantial, Cotignola. Hawkwood became extremely enamoured of his new home on which he lavished much time and money. He enlarged and strengthened the fortifications to the existing castle, converted the bell tower of the church into a watch tower and generally embellished the fortification.

Nearby was the home of the future founder of the house of Sforza, who succeeded the Visconti as Lords of Milan in 1450. Maybe young Muzio Attendolo Sforza picked up some useful tips in his childhood from observing the practices of the neigbouring English general.

The castle stayed in Hawkwood's possession until 1381. The ditches and strong bastioned walls with which surrounded the town remained almost intact until the middle of the 19th century. Now all that is left is the single round tower.

Neighbouring Bagnocavallo later achieved fame as the place where Byron's much loved daughter, Allegra, died in a convent school.

A shameful episode

The general insurrection against the papacy now moved up to Bologna and Hawkwood was despatched to try and take the town of Granarola. Here again he failed against the populace, under their commander Astore Manfredi.

Meanwhile the city of Faenza called upon Hawkwood to protect its citizens. It had been ceded to the papacy in 1356 but in 1375 the citizens rebelled and joined the Florentine League. Now they were fearful of papal reprisals. The city's importance lay in the fact that, although in the plain, it is situated at the entrance of the Val di Lamone and thus the meeting point of many major routes across the peninsula. By the 1370s the city was also already beginning to acquire a reputation for the manufacture of glazed earthenware, a ceramic whose generic term, majolica, derived from Majorca where it was invented, but whose local name became celebrated as "faenza" and in France as "faience".

Hawkwood, still under contract to the papacy, preferred to obey the instructions of his patron to suppress the rebellion and regain Faenza for his master. Ignoring the pleas of the citizens he entered the city crushing the rebellious citizens with brute force. Contemporary accounts describe some details of the atrocities committed by Hawkwood's troops. The population was disarmed on pain of a fine and corporal punishment. The old men and women and children were driven out of the town. There was mass raping of both virgins and matrons, even a duel between two English constables over a nun, which Hawkwood is alleged to have solved in the style of Solomon by dividing the spoils. This story though probably fictitious is a measure of the feelings of horror in which contemporaries held the English behaviour in the battle. It is certainly true that the carnage was overwhelming, the city stripped bare and the remaining population annihilated. The only explanation, but certainly no justification, of his behaviour is that Hawkwood was desperate for money and that no doubt his hungry troops had overindulged on the produce of the vanquished, driving their actions beyond reason.

History has laid the opprobrium at Hawkwood's feet but recently Stephen Cooper in "Chivalry and the Art of War" has suggested that possibly Faenza may have already been in a state of siege by the Florentines, which Hawkwood and his men were called in to raise. Even if the blame for these horrific deeds can be partially apportioned to Florence it is no excuse for his actions.

Bologna was very tempted to make reprisals but luckily refrained. However it did decide to abandon its allegiance to the pope and join the Florentine League. In so doing they imprisoned all the English in the city including children amongst whom were two figures referred to as "Hawkwood's sons". Existing records only show evidence of daughters by his first wife, and there is only reference to the existence of one natural son, so to whom this refers is a subject of speculation.

At the end of this shameful episode having milked Faenza

dry on behalf of the Pope, Hawkwood ceded it for 60,000 ducats to Alberto d' Este, Marquis of Ferrara, and retired to his beloved Cotignola to enjoy the summer. One wonders whether Hawkwood did not then toy with the idea of returning home to England. He did seek a general pardon from the english parliament to ease any future return to England and, presumably, to make retribution of any wrongs he had committed in previous years in France and the peninsula. However this was not to be. He was left in little peace and was constantly being wooed by both Florence and the papacy. Florence, Bologna and Milan joined together in a secret resolve to break up the english company by offering the soldiers higher pay.

The Papacy betrayed

The neighbouring city of Cesena was another papal state suffering from local insurrection, also quite possibly instigated by Florentine supporters behind the scenes. It was ruled over by the powerful and cruel Swiss cardinal Roberto, Count of Geneva , who was leader of the Breton group with whom Hawkood had fought with little success against the townsfolk of Forli.

In the summer of 1376 Roberto decided to turn his attention towards his own townsmen. Perhaps it was an act of desperation on behalf of the papacy. Many of their former territories were joining in the fast spreading insurresion against the Church and were difficult to control from Avignon. The catalyst which the cardinal seized upon was an argument over food. The cardinal had given his Breton soldiers the right to requisition victuals from the townspeople who, understandably, were retaliating. As a result these ruthless Breton soldiers set about plundering the shops and causing havoc in the city. The row finally flared up over an attempted theft from a local butchers shop, by a group of Bretons. All havoc broke loose and the cardinal found the situation becoming beyond his control. In the full heat of the August sun he summoned Hawkwood to his aid.

Ostensibly Hawkwood, still under allegiance to the pope was beholden to accede to this request. The cardinal conceived a plan whereby he would trick the citizens with promises of peace and indulgences in return for laying down their arms. To present day ears this proposition might not have much appeal but, in an era when hell fire was greatly feared, indulgences were a much sought after commodity. The cardinal had no intention of keeping his word and having de-armed the citizens intended to slaughter them mercilessly. Hawkwood was at first extremely unwilling to assist at such an orgy of mass destruction on largely innocent people. His own philosophy of warfare favoured expelling populations then plundering their city, rather than killing the citizens. With great reluctance he finally agreed. It is claimed however, that before the battle commenced, he managed to evacuate a thousand women and children to nearby Rimini.

Even so the total of human deaths in this bloody massacre in the
name of the pope was estimated between three and eight thousand
defenceless men and women. This act of destruction lasted for
three nights and three days. As well as the enormous loss of
human life the whole fabric of the city was largely destroyed.
What we see today is chiefly a fifteenth century reconstruction
carried out by Galeotto Malatesta to whom the subsequent pope,
Urban VI, eventually ceded the city.

   Contemporaries probably viewed Hawkwood's
participation in these atrocitities with less disgust than us today.
After all a condottiere's duty was to fight for his master of the
moment and not take sides. The full extent that Florence played
in stirring up these rebellions against the papacy, and how much
they were the cause of these horrific battles, is not to be dismissed
and yet to be documented.

   The "St.Bartholomew Night" of Cesena was the last
service Hawkwood and his company performed for the papacy.
He left their services in disgust some weeks later and accepted the
generalship of the Florentine Confederacy to which Milan had
now become affiliated.

A Visconti bride

By 1377 Bernabo Visconti was a very influential member of the
Florentine Confederacy and not only offered to provide half the
fee negotiated by Hawkwood in this new association but also
offered him the hand in marriage of one of his illegitimate
daughters. Donnina was the daughter of Donnina de Porri, a
milanese noblewoman and famous beauty of her time.
Estimates vary as to the number of children sired by this vigorous
potentate. The usually accepted figure is thirty-six, of which
fifteen were by his wife, a member of the Scala family of Verona,
and the remaining thirty-one by local ladies of rank. Little
distinction was made in the rearing of this vast progeny.

Whereas Bernabo preferred to marry off his legitimate
daughters to princes of the blood royal, he found it highly
expedient to choose husbands for his bastards on the distaff side
among the leading soldiers of fortune. In this way he could exert
some pull over the condottieri concerned. Although Hawkwood
had proved himself to be his own man with no intention of
becoming Bernabo's tool, it is easy to understand the advantage he
thought this alliance would bring to the Milanese.

With such an extensive progeny it is not surprising that the
Visconti family still abounds today Perhaps Bernabo's most
famous descendant in recent history is the celebrated film director

Luchino Visconti whose works include The Leopard [1963] and
Death in Venice [1973].

What was in it for Hawkwood? First of all there was a
very welcome income of 10,000 florins. Secondly By 1376 he is
referred to in contemporary accounts as a widower, so we must
assume that his first wife had deceased somewhere along the line
leaving him alone and perhaps lonely, without a mother for his
children or a wife to run his newly acquired castle. Alas no
archive informs us as to whether Hawkwood's English wife and
family followed him to Italy or what befell them. It was not
unusual for wives to join their husbands abroad at the time and
one likes to assume that Hawkwood's desire to return home
would have been more noticeable if she had been left behind.
There is a legend that his English wife settled with her children at
Pisa but what became of her is unknown. Their daughter
Antiocha is recorded as marrying in Milan in 1379 William de
Coggeshall from Essex, and another daughter Fiorentina as
marrying a certain Lancilloto del Maino which suggests they must
have lived in the peninsula.

Meanwhile money, and the need to earn it, kept him
fighting. Hawkwood had reached a position of immense personal
power in north and central Italy, with all allied states making
payments of fees totalling 250,000 florins a year just to buy
immunity from his aggression. He cannot therefore have failed to
be flattered by this crown to his success. Also with his evident
growing attachment to the country this alliance with Bernabo's
daughter would change his status from just another foreign

condottiere. He was already the landowner of a strong castle with fertile lands and now he was the son-in-law of the most powerful autocrat in the peninsula, paid by half of Italy and honourably bound for life to the strong republic of Florence.

How well the couple knew each other before the event, or if at all, is not recorded. Hawkwood was already fifty-seven and Donnina probably not even twenty, but it does emerge that Hawkwood was fond and faithful to his bride and, despite his age, sired from her one son and three daughters. From the little we know of his private life it appears that he was devoted to his family and not given to the wild profligacy of other condottieri of the time. I have only found one reference suggesting any untowards behaviour.

Another consideration in Hawkwood's agreement to this alliance may well have been the deteriorating situation in England where his elderly patron and sovereign, Edward III, after years of successful rule, was enduring an impoverished and dishonoured old age. His queen, Philippa, had died in 1369 since when he had sunk into deep depression and taken up with a woman of ill repute called Alice Perrers, under whose unscrupulous sway he was ruling these last years of his life. Meanwhile he had milked his subjects dry to pay for his endless wars. He was imposing tax after tax on his subjects culminating in the imposition of a poll-tax of a groat a head which lead to the Peasants Revolt. Any desire by Hawkwood to return home may have been cast aside.

The marriage with Donina was arranged for May 1377. Bernabo, for whom it was an oportunity to display his own power and wealth, did Hawkwood proud over the wedding ceremonies. These were shared by another of his illegitimate daughters, Elizabeth, whom he married off to the german condottiere, Count Lucius Landau, commander of the Star Company. Hawkwood and he joined forces for some time after their respective marriages.

The Mantuan Ambassador at the court of Milan sent back the following description of the wedding day to Luigi Gonzaga: *"Sir John Achud on Sunday last took his wife home with much honour to the house in which the Bishop of Parma used to live and at the nuptials were present, the Lady Duchess and all the children of Lord Bernabo, together with an honourable company. After dinner, Lord Bernabo went with Porina [the bride's mother] to Sir John`s house where there was jousting all day. I am told that the Lady Regina [Bernabo's wife] presented the bride with a thousand gold ducats in a cup. Marco [Bernabo's eldest son] gave her a string of pearls worth 300 ducats and his brother Luigi gave her a pearl necklace of the same value and many people of rank did the like. The English also presented her with a quantity of silver which is estimated at 1,000 ducats. There was no dancing out of respect for the memory of Thaddeo...."*

After honeymooning in Cremona Hawkwood returned to work in his new capacity as General of the Florentine Confederacy. This gave him the scope to fight where called upon as long as the interests of the confederacy were not endangered, and on the proviso that he should come whenever Florence beckoned. His first assignments were local where he was sent to

Dear Both,

I so much enjoyed
seeing Nicholas at P.J.
Only sad to miss Tom.

Here's a copy of our
book. Festive report, 1987
what I have connected
some of my earlier
love
Katie

an

e

39406/37780

ne.com

extract from Bologna their dues owing to the confederacy of 30,000 florins. They refused to give Hawkwood either passage or provisions – let alone the money – so he was forced to plunder the surrounding countryside to maintain his troops. Florence tried to intervene to no avail and Hawkwood was forced to withdraw. In those far off days armies provided no supply trains and depended on foraging by gift or stealth from the surrounding countryside for their subsistence. This was viewed as fair payment if your city was being defended, but if it was under attack was considered as plunder.

In a gesture that must have gone some way to salve his conscience Hawkwood then helped Astore Manfredi to recover the city of Faenza, which he had so shamelessly ransacked the previous year. The chief source of resistance to the Florentine League was a company of Bretons who were causing havoc in the towns of the Po valley in Cesena. Heading this force was a nephew of Pope Gregory, Raimondo, whom Hawkwood succeeded in preventing from crossing the Tiber, forcing him to take his troops to raise a siege of the Maremma in the west.

Hawkwood himself wintered at San Quirico near Siena with whose Ambassador he was on good terms. He passed the two months of the late autumn 1377 trying to mediate for peace between the Florentine League and the Church, and receiving endless overtures from Sienese ambassadors who tempted him with many bribes. Alas, the peace negotiations finally broke down. In December when Hawkwood marched his troops into Florence, although he was received with due respect and

appropriate celebrations, his peace proposals were not well
entertained. He himself only tarried a few days in the city
returning to Cotignola and his new wife for Christmas.
Meanwhile his troops remained foraging in florentine territory
which, although part of the agreement, was not very popular with
the locals.

Birth of a schism

As 1378 dawned the stalemate between the papacy and the
Florentine League remained unresolved. Although Pope Gregory
had finally managed to return to Rome, in January the previous
year he was only able to establish himself in the Vatican near the
tomb of St. Peter, rather than in the basilica of Saint John Lateran
where his predecessors had resided. Bernabo Visconti now set out
to try his hand at settling a peace between the two parties. To this
effect he entrusted to his English son-in-law, a stalwart warrior
and respected diplomat, the delicate task of escorting the papal
delegates to their rendezvous with the Visconti at Sarzanna. The
delegates consisted of the Cardinal of Amiens and the Archbishops
of Pamplona and Narbonne. Thanks to Hawkwood's connections
with Siena he was able to procure from the city safe conduct for
these papal delegates and for his troops to pass through their lands.
Unfortunately any progress Visconti made towards treaties with
the papacy was opposed by Florence.

Exhausted and stricken bythe continuous plots going on

around him Pope Gregory died on March 27th 1378 at the age of forty-seven. Any peace talks were forced to go on hold. All eyes were on Rome and the election of a new pontiff. The College of Cardinals was mainly composed of Frenchmen. They realised they were not popular in Italy and that it would be unwise for this position, which carried not only spiritual but also strong secular power, to go to one of their compatriots. In the event a compromise was reached by electing a neapolitan cardinal. Although by birth from the peninsula, he was a subject of the French Angevins who ruled the Kingdom of Naples. The solution seemed acceptable to both the French and Italians. Bartolomeo Prignano, Urban VI as he styled himself, enjoyed a short period of popularity but did manage to make peace with the Florentine League on July 24th, the feast of St. John the Baptist their patron saint.

Soon after his election Pope Urban's character appeared to change – or perhaps his true character emerged. His life had been austere and he was known as a strong supporter of reform. Now his tactless and tyrannical manner speedily alienated the very cardinals who had elected him, and earned him the nickname of *inurbino*, meaning "the rude one". Even St. Catherine of Siena, one of his most loyal supporters wrote to him:

"For the love of Jesus crucified, Holy Father, soften a little the sudden movements of your temper."

Slowly the opposition of the cardinals grew. Urban tried to win them back, which only provoked them to make a declaration doubting whether the election had been valid. By the

85

time the thirteen cardinals met together at Forli later that
year, they unanimously voted for a rival, or Anti-Pope, in the
person of the diabolical Robert of Geneva, the Butcher of Cesena,
who took the name of Clement VII.

Urban at once took up arms against him, and Clement was
forced to flee to Avignon where he established his rival seat, thus
begetting a schism that divided the Church throughout the
Christian world. The roman pope Urban, despite his character,
was supported by the majority of his countrymen along with
northern Europe including England, whilst the Anti-Pope was
supported by France and the south. This situation created political
unrest throughout Europe which continued for forty years.

Enter Geoffrey Chaucer

Edward III died in June 1376. The Black Prince, his talented and
promising heir, had predeceased his father by a year, dying of an
unknown illness in France, leaving the throne to his ten year old
son, who became Richard II. During his minority the throne
was left in the hands of his uncle, the younger brother of the Black
Prince, the Duke of Lancaster, known as John of Gaunt after the
city of Ghent where he was born.

King Edward had left his country in a state of poverty and
resulting social unrest. There were continuing conflicts in

Parliament and deep suspicions on the part of Londoners and others of the motives of John of Gaunt. The exchequer was drained empty by the expenses of war. The political and economic scenes were far from stable. Peace with France seemed hard to come by on any permanent basis. Enmity between the two countries was now further increased by the schism in the papacy, over which France and England had divided loyalties.

This was the background against which John of Gaunt took the decision to send an embassy to Milan in 1378. England, who now had a further alliance with Northern Italy behind the new roman pope, probably hoped to take advantage of this opportunity to treat and to borrow funds from the coffers of the Visconti. The ambassadors entrusted with this mission were Sir Edward Berkeley attended by Geoffrey Chaucer. Their brief ostensibly was to take the king's greetings to Bernabo Visconti, lord of Milan and *"nostre cher et foial Sir John Hawkwood "* and to treat with them of business to do with the king's wars. This is a clear illustration of how Hawkwood's standing and affiliation with the Milanese, coupled with his dedication to his own sovereign, was such a useful diplomatic card for the English to play.

There was also a hidden agenda to endeavour to obtain the hand of Bernabo's daughter, Caterina, for the young English king Richard II. By now 12 years of age Richard was one of the most eligible bachelors on the royal and political scene of Europe. Relations between Milan and England had remained close despite the untimely death of the Duke of Clarence after his short marriage to Violante Visconti in 1368. They had been further cemented by their alliance with the English mercenary through his marriage with Donnina Visconti, and it was probably through Hawkwood that Bernabo transmitted his interest in the match for Caterina. It could result in great prestige for the Milanese and much needed wealth for the impoverished English monarchy.

How does Chaucer enter the scene? He gained access to the royal household through his father, who was a vintner and deputy to King Edward III's Butler. He was bright, and used his position to study. Having a penchant for poetry he probably made himself popular with the ladies of the court whom he pleased with his ditties. He fell into the role of part courtier responsible for entertaining the court with his poetry, and part civil servant owing to his intelligence and command of English, French and Latin. It must have been this knowledge and learning which led to him being used on diplomatic missions abroad.

Chaucer had accompanied two previous embassies to Genoa. The brief of the first in 1372 was to treat with the doge about a suitable port for the importation of English wool. His second brief was a secret mission to Florence, probably to secure even more loans for King Edward from the Florentine bankers. Whatever business he carried out must have been successful as on his return the king awarded his *"dilecto Armigero Galfrido Chaucer"* a daily pitcher of wine, and appointed him Controller of the Customs covering the subsidy on wools, skins and hides in the Port of London. This position carried much power as wool was England's most important export.

The impression and influence on Chaucer of these foreign

visits must have been tremendous and emerges in some of his tales. Like Hawkwood, Chaucer must have been dazzled by the beauty, opulence and comparative comfort of Italian domestic architecture, the beauty of her landscape, the art of her craftsmen and of course her great libraries.

With this experience before him, and now under the patronage of John of Gaunt, Chaucer made the ideal choice as a member of this further embassy to Italy to treat with Milan. Undoubtedly Chaucer and Hawkwood would have had much to discuss, and Hawkwood must have enjoyed catching up on news from the homeland. Chaucer, for his part, would have greatly enjoyed the opportunity of visiting the magnificent libraries of both Bernabo and Galeazzo Visconti in Milan and Pavia. It may well have been Galeazzo who introduced him to, or obtained for him, copies of the works of the great Italian writer, Boccaccio, which were to have such a profound influence on his own writing. Both these ruthless tyrants harboured a passion for manuscripts and were generous patrons of the arts. If one considers them in the light of the time, both anxious to manifest their power and wealth, as so many military and political figures have done before and after them, it is understandable.

With the emerging interest in classical texts throughout Europe which was to inspire the "humanist movement" men offwealth, who aspired to learning, competed with each other to collect manuscripts both ancient and contemporary on subjects which hitherto had been considered pagan. As such they had been banned by the papacy and therefore neglected. With the more liberal attitude which was fast becoming fashionable they were being re-examined. Galeazzo died during Chaucer`s visit so, alas, they did not meet. However evidently Bernabo left a lasting impression on him as when some years later he came to write the Monk's Tale Chaucer cited him as a tragic victim of false fortune after he was deposed by his nephew.

What truth there is in the idea that Chaucer based his knight in the Knight's Tale on Hawkwood is still a subject of speculation. Certainly the chivalrous qualities of the knight in question, which Chaucer describes,do evoke what Hawkwood's admirers could interpret as a his portrait:

> *A Knight there was– and that a worthy man–*
> *That from the time that he first began*
> *To riden out, he loved chivalrye,*
> *Trouth and honour, freedom and curteisye.*
> *Full worthy was he in his lordes were,*
> *And thereto had he riden, no man ferre,*
> *As well in Cjristendome as in heathenesse,*
> *And ever honoured for his worthinesse*

The achievements of Berkeley and Chaucer on this visit unfortunately are unrecorded. A group of Milanese councillors did return with the English envoy to continue discussions about the marriage proposal. These were sufficiently advanced for the English to send a second embassy to Milan to work out details of a marriage treaty in 1379 but their negotiaitons seem to have come to an abrupt halt when one of their number returned to London. The other two councillors proceeded to Rome where the affair appears to have fizzled out. Possibly the chaos caused by the schism excluded any opportunity for negotiations of this nature. Ultimately the marriage plans between the young English king Richard II and Bernabo's daughter Caterina came to nothing.

Mission to Verona

Later in 1378, after the English Embassy had departed empty handed, Bernabo Visconti decided to deploy Hawkwood, with his other son–in–law Lucius Landau, on his own diplomatic mission. He despatched them, in the name of his wife Beatrice, to claim the city of Verona as her lawful inheritance from her brother, Signore della Scala. They were highly successful and managed to take over the city refraining from inflicting any bloodshed, in exchange for a down payment from Verona of four hundred thousand golden florins and the promise of an annual tribute of forty thousand for six years. This appears a very expensive treaty for the Veronese, but obviously they were persuaded that to enter battle would be a worse option. It was yet another token of Hawkwood's powers of negotiation and of his military reputation.   The two brothers in–law were not quite so successful in their efforts to protect Venice from the threat of the the Anti–Venetian league which was headed by the Marquis of Padua, supported by Hungary and the Republic of Genoa. Fearful perhaps of strong opposition the allies refused to enter battle despite the fee of 30,000 gold ducats proffered to them. Moreover, when they re–entered veronese territory later in the summer, they were ignominiously defeated during an encounter with the Hungarian army. Bernabo was forced to call a 45 day truce.

Hostilities were resumed in December. This time the allies managed to advance to within six miles of Verona before yet again being defeated by the Hungarians and forced to retreat with heavy losses. Bernabo disillusioned by their performance cut off their wages and accused them of shirking a fight. This was understandably badly received by Hawkwood and his allies. The troops indemnified themselves by pillaging the Visconti property of Bresciano.

Consequently relationships between father–in–law and son–in–law soured and Hawkwood decided to take leave of Bernabo's service. What his wife Donnina thought about this enmity between father and husband we can only surmise. Perhaps she was accustomed to such political somersaults since all was considered fair in warfare.

Florentine social unrest

It is difficult to exaggerate the impact the Plague, or Black Death as it was known in England, had made on the population of northern Europe. It first erupted in 1348, recurring at ten or twenty year intervals till 1400. The population was reduced by half. Many cities in Italy lost a third of their townsfolk. The physical symptoms of the disease were terrifying: violent fever, sweating, delirium, unbearable thirst, discoloration of the skin and swellings the size of eggs in the groin or armpit. During these outbreaks the healthy abandoned their families in terrified attempts to save themselves, leaving the bodies of the afflicted piled up in the streets. The stench and sanitary conditions of the townships gave rise to further disease. Even worse were the psychological effects. The plague came close to breaking down the whole fabric of medieval society. Ignorant of the cause of this unheralded affliction, the common man imagined it to be a punishment imposed by the Almighty on an erring people.

Furthermore the 1370s had been a decade of manifold troubles for the Republic of Florence. 1371 had seen yet another outbreak of the Plague and the bad harvest of 1373 had caused severe shortages of food. The papal ban on the import of wheat from Romagna in 1376 further exacerbated the situation. The flourishing slave trade indirectly augmented the number of unemployed. It was cheaper to buy a slave than pay a regular wage. Flemish cloth began to rival in quality that of Florence, thus introducing unwelcome competition to what had been almost a monopoly of this most important industry.

Three of Florence's leading banking houses went bankrupt: the Peruzzi, the Acciaiuoli and the Bardi. This was largely due to Edward III of England on whom they relied to supply the raw wool for their cloth trade. Having built up good relations with the italian banks, King Edward turned to them to borrow money for his wars. Repayment of these loans was not always forthcoming. As some banks were wont to lend up to 14 times their share capital perhaps their collapse was not surprising!

The war with the papacy was still unresolved. In 1376 Pope Gregory XI had laid an interdict on Florence, which the local clergy totally ignored. His Holiness had also ordered all Christian rulers to expel Florentine merchants from their lands. It was even decreed licit to rob them!

To handle the drastic economic situation Florence appointed eight emergency governors who were called the "Otto Santi" – the eight saints. With the death of Gregory XI in 1378 Florence and the advent of new Roman Pontiff, Urban VI, these two powers had a mutual interest in making peace; Florence on account of the disruption to its trade, and Urban on account of the insecurity of his position threatened by the election of the anti-Pope.

The increased levy of taxes led to social and political unrest. That same year the crisis burst into civil strife with "the Ciompi Revolt". Ciompi was the onomatopoeic nickname of the washers and carders of wool, derived from the sound of the clomping of their clogs. They formed the lowest order of the largest florentine guild, Arte della Lana. and were known as the "popolo minuto". Encouraged by Salvestro de Medici, their Gonfaloniere of Justice, who was seeking to maintain his own predominance in government, this upsurge of violence forced the Otto Santi to resign. The Balia, or Special Commission, which took their place included 32 men specifically designated to be chosen from the Ciompi, with one of their members elected as Gonfaloniere of Justice. Unfortunately the people could not cope with the ropes of government for long, and a new oligarchy emerged who made few concessions to the lower orders.

During this period Hawkwood had been busy with the business of the Visconti in Milan. In fact he was never called upon by Florence to intercede in her internal political affairs. Probably they were fearful lest, as was common amongst other condottieri of the time, he should wish to make himself master of the city through a show of strength. They need not have worried as, unlike his peers, Hawkwood was totally uninterested in politics or power and hoped for nothing more than a comfortable old age. As Scipio Amirato was to write:

"...by many proofs he [Hawkwood] showed himself valiant and courageous in his own person, astute in reaping advantages and a man who could wait the results of action without hurrying to obtain fame. "

Hawkwood, however, never lost touch with Florence as is witnessed from the fact that he persuaded the city reluctantly to pay 2,000 florins to an emissary whom he discovered was privy to plans of a counter offensive in the city by the guelph party. Thanks to this bribe the emissary revealed the plans to Hawkwood and Florence was able to counteract the plot. Any doubts Florence might have held about Hawkwood's integrity must have surely thereby been expelled.

The crown of Naples

Sicily, Naples and its hinterland were an independent Kingdom under the rule of the French Angevins, and was referred to colloquially by the inhabitants of the north as the "Reame". During an incident on Easter Monday 1282, known as the Sicilian Vespers, the French inhabitants of Sicily were massacred and thrown out of the island by the Arogans from Spain, leaving the Angevins with only Naples. Over subsequent years the French spent much of their resources and energy in trying to repossess the Sicily. Despite the efforts of the illustrious and wise French king, Robert of Anjou, trade in the "Reame" gradually declined and civil unrest ensued.

Robert died in 1343 and the crown passed to his 16 year old grand-daughter Giovanna. Queen Giovanna had suffered since childhood from a retarded mental disorder which rendered her very unstable. Indeed she was known as Giovanna *pazza*, Giovanna the mad. Despite her condition she was married off to Andrew Durazzo, Prince of Hungary. The marriage did not last long as the poor bridegroom met an untimely death at the hands of an assassin in 1345. Andrew's brother, King Louis of Hungary, assuming the collective guilt of the Neapolitan Court and the necessity of revenge, invaded the *Reame* in the hope of securing it for himself. In this endeavour however he was unsuccessful. As a result Naples was left without a competent leader and there ensued a massive breakdown of law and order which gave rise to an open invitation for all foreign mercenary companies in the peninsula to rampage throughout the *Reame*.

Somehow Giovanna herself survived and we find her by 1382 a fanatic supporter of the new French anti-pope, Clement VII, and his court of french cardinals. As such she was at odds with the majority of the peninsula who were behind the roman pope Urban VI. In the struggle against her Pope Urban called on the assistance of Charles Durazzo, nephew of King Louis of Hungary, and therefore by marriage also of Giovanna, on whom he took it upon himself to confer the crown of Naples. The anti-pope, Clement VII, intervened by sending to Naples the brother of King CharlesV of France, Louis of Anjou, whom the queen had previsously designated and favoured as her successor. Louis of Anjou with an army of picked soldiers and the help of King Amadeo VI of Savoy crossed the river Po and threatened all the tuscan states hostile to the anti-pope Clement VII.

Milan appealed to King Louis of Hungary for protection in a letter, written by Petrarch, in the name of Bernabo Visconti. Florence turned to Hawkwood to protect her against the threat of these French invaders. She offered him five hundred lances to assist him, 130,000 florins for six months service, plus an

additional 1,000 florins as Hawkwood`s personal salary.
He accepted and protected the city with such success that the
terms of engagement were thrice renewed.

Hawkwood's protection of Florence against the French
Angevin usurper of the Neopolitan crown earned him official
recognition by the city. In 1383, he was appointed its Captain
General. This post carried enormous prestige both in terms of
military command and legal jurisdiction.   It had never before
been held by a foreigner to Florence, let alone a foreigner of the
peninsula.   Hawkwood accepted the Baton "in the name of God".
His appointment marked the beginning of Hawkwood's
permanent affiliation with Florence, which was to last until his
death. He was re–elected continuously in the post until in 1391 he
was created Captain General for Life, and an Honorary Citizen of
Florence.

Pope Urban subsequently requested the Florentine
government to place Hawkwood at the disposal of Charles
Durazzo, their candidate for the crown of Naples.   Florence
refused to involve itself further, but did allow Hawkwood, on his
own account, to accompany Charles with two thousand horses to
the *Reame*. The armies headed south and eventually reached
Naples. Here Charles lost no time in imprisoning the poor mad
queen and subsequently had her put to death. In April 1383 the
Duke of Anjou died. However the battle for Naples was by no
means over. The cudgels were taken up anew by young Anjou
and young Durazzo. Despite the efforts of the Hungarians and
their allies, the *Reame* remained under Angevin domination until

1442 when taken over by the Spanish Aroganese.

Thinking his services in the *Reame* were no longer needed and that he had fulfilled his obligations Hawkwood withdrew from the scene to return to his beloved tuscany. In his capacity as Captain General of Florence Hawkwood passed much time over the next few years protecting tuscan states from the French marauders whilst simultaneously supporting Charles Durazzo against his rivals on behalf of the Pope. An illustration of the awe and fear which he engendered is the monthly fee of 100 florins Siena were forced to pay him to keep off their land. Of course his services to the Pope had to be agreed by Florence under the terms of his contract with the city, and did not come without their fees.

In his advance through Italy Charles Durazzo conquered and took over the city of Arezzo, a major stronghold among the tuscan states. This was a little awkward for Florence who dearly wished to have the city under its own control but who, on the other hand, was beholden to protecting Charles. The latter proved to be very severe on the citizens who spent four years groaning under the yoke of his rule. In 1384 he was ousted by a French company sent by Louis d'Anjou, under the command of Enguerrand VII Sire de Coucy. This event liberated Florence to make an overture to obtain Arezzo for themselves. Several months of negotiations ensued culminating in the French being persuaded to sell Arezzo back to Florence for ready money, without the cost of any lives. An unusual feat in those days of bloodshed. Charles Durazzo was eventually murdered in 1386.

Landlord of Montecchio

Hawkwood's relationship with Florence did not always run smoothly. He was greatly irritated, for instance, by her delay in producing the agreed sums for the purchase of his house in Florence in which he was anxious to settle his family now he was working in the south. He also resented their lack of support in his dispute with Astore Manfredi over the city of Granarola. In fact relations became so soured that he decided to abscond his position as Captain General of Florence and join a combined German and Hungarian company. On hearing this Florence was desperate enough to send an embassy to Hawkwood, who extracted an agreement from him to break his new alliance for a sum of 5,000 florins. This having been settled, and amicable relations restored, Hawkwood allowed himself to be re-elected Captain General of Florence.

The rich city of Arezzo, after being much fought over and racked by internal conflicts, was now an independent commune. In 1336 it was sold to Florence by one of the influential Tarlati family who had controlled it for thirty odd years but managed to regain its independence in 1342, which it kept until 1384. It was then captured by the French Enguerrand VII Lord de Coucy, who in turn had sold the city to Florence. Hawkwood, as Captain General of Florence, was thus left the undisputed Military Lord of

Tuscany, affording him some breathing space between battles to see to his own affairs. He had already sold his Cotignola estate to the Marchese d`Este for 60,000 ducats in 1381. Much as he loved it, now that he had left the service of the Visconti and his military activities were centred around tuscany, the distance from Florence no longer made it practical. To leave his family there unprotected would have been unsafe. For this reason he moved them to Florence where he negotiated with the city for funds to purchase a house. The funds were eventually forthcoming.

As Captain General of Florence Hawkwood was not allowed not to absent himself over eighty miles from the city, but he did not lose his desire for a country estate of his own. By the mid 1380s he was the proprietor of a large domain south of Arezzo in the middle of, what had now become, his main field of operations only 50 miles from Florence

Standing on a hillock north of Cortona dominating to the west the plain leading to Siena, and to the south the plain as far as Lake Trasimeno, stands the towering castle of Montecchio. Even now it strikes wonder and awe into the hearts of its beholders. The position is such that no fourteenth century cavalry or infantry battalion would have been able to approach unnoticed. Hawkwood of course knew the area well from his endless skirmishes with Siena and other city states in the neighbourhood. Apart from its numerous military advantages and the provision of good shelter for his troops, he had fallen in love with tuscany, as so many Englishmen to follow,

The exact date of Hawkwood's acquisition is unknown.

Some historians have hypothesised that the castle came into Hawkwood's possession as early as 1375, but this is highly unlikely as he was busily engaged elsewhere and still owned Cotignola at the time. Moreover Montecchio still belonged to Arezzo. Also from an entry in a book belonging to the neighbouring town of Castiglion Fiorentino, dated November 29th 1380 which was still under the rule of Arezzo, we know the commune authorised the payment of a sum of money for the maintenance of Montecchio to a certain Giovanni di Grinta described as "the custodian". Had the property belonged to Hawkwood at this date Castiglion Fiorentino certainly would not have been contributing towards the running expenses. Nor does it feature in the work of the contemporary poet, Gorello, when lamenting the properties which had passed out of the city's jurisdiction into the hands of local nobles and communes between 1380 and 1381. By June 1384 Montecchio appears amongst the properties declared by the powerful Tarlati family of Arezzo as their exclusive possessions, and, as such, recommended to the commune of Siena in the act of submission to the latter, signed by Cardinal Galeotto Tarlati and his brothers. Together with Montecchio in the same document is Migliari, which is definitely recorded as the property of Acuto at the time. Perhaps the Tarlatti had included in their list of submission all the properties over which they had ancient rights, but not necessarily current control, which could have applied to Montecchio. However, in view of the dramas besetting the Tarlati at that moment this view seems a little unlikely. What is certain is that in that same year, 1384, Florence was apologising to Acuto for not replying to his request concerning a property which he was occupying and which he had offered for sale to Florence. With the fall of Arezzo the balance of power in the region had changed, and it is most probable that it was after this event in early 1385 when Montecchio was freed from its Aretine masters that it was acquired by Hawkwood .

In addition to the military advantages of owning this magnificent fortress, and his love of the local countryside, maybe Hawkwood also desired a castle of his own as a status symbol. He had recently been appointed the english King Richard II's Ambassador to the Papal Court, along with Sir Nicolas Dagworth and Johannes Bacon. As such, they had been given full powers to conclude commercial treaties with Naples, Florence and other Italian states. These treaties covered all manner of trade deals between the two countries and chiefly concerned the import of wool, the major subject of barter at the time, for which the english king had recently signed a new agreement. We know that Hawkwood was probably in residence in 1386 during the raid of Cortona, and there is a letter dated 1387 from the Signoria of Florence to the Podesta of Castiglion Fiorentino requesting free passaage for three loads of arms and armour which Acuto wished to despatch through their territories.

From the little one can glean, Hawkwood's wife and family settled happily at their new abode. It was a safe and agreeable place in which to bring up children. There is a record of a property tax demand in April 1386 made out in the name of Donnina giving her fifteen days in which to pay. This suggests that the running of the estate largely fell on her shoulders as her husband was so often absent, engaged on his own military affairs.

Handed down to us are one or two anecdotes from the time of Hawkwood's ownership. The first records an instance when two friars going about their business from one castle to another found themselves at Montecchio, hardly a mile from Cortona, and coming into his [Acuto's] presence, according to their custom said " Monsignore, God grant you peace". He immediately replied "May the Almighty rob you of your alms! " The friars, almost fainting in surpise, said "Sir, why do you speak thus?" Signor Giovanni replied "Also you, why do you speak like that to me?" Said the friars "We believed we were pronouncing a blessing." And signor Giovanni replied "How can you believe you bring me a blessing, when you come and ask that God should make me die of hunger? Do you not know that I live by war, and that peace does not suit me at all? So as I live by war, you live by begging; and yes the reply, which I have given you, is similar to your salutation." The friars shrugged their shoulders and said "Signore you are right, forgive us, we are simple people". And having nothing more to do with him they parted and returned to the convent of Castiglione Aretino. They esteemed the incident worthy of a new short story, not specially for "Messer Giovanni August", but for those who wished to remain in peace. For sure he was the most hard man of arms in Italy. A hardy sixty year old, with almost all cities paying tribute to him, well he knew that there was little peace in Italy in his times.

Another anecdote recounts how, in the summer of 1388,

Acuto saved the life of his brother-in-law, Carlo Visconti, from a poison plot whilst at Cortona. The incident took place at the residence of Uguccio Casali, lord of Cortona, with whom Carlo Visconti was staying. Gian Galeazzo Visconti his cousin, who had just become Lord of Milan, was trying to eliminate all of his relations who in his view could remove him from power. In this connection he bribed a doctor from Casali, Messer Gioioso, with a sum of 30,000 florins to poison both Carlo and his host Uguccio. One morning Gioioso visited Carlo and, with the excuse of the heavy summer air, tried to persuade him, for the benefit of his health, to eat certain figs and drink certain wine, both of which had been poisoned. Carlo Visconti was warned of the plot by Giovanni Acuto who got wind of it in neighbouring Montecchio and immediately informed Casali, asking him if one of his faithful doctors would ever carry out a such crime. Casali forced the doctor to confess, promising him pardon. However once the confession had been extracted, the doctor was tied down on to a cart, tortured and quartered. His quarters were hung on the people's gate of Cortona as a warning to other potential scoundrels with the same idea. Death by poison was one of the most common and feared ways of asasination in those times. As a resulting precaution the rich and powerful seldom ate food presented to them at table which had not previously been tasted by one of their henchmen.

The leopard shows his spots

The relative peace of life at Montecchio was rudely interrupted in
May 1385. Acuto's father- in- law, Bernabo Visconti, was
unexpectedly overthrown by his young nephew Giangaleazzo,
the son of his brother Galeazzo. The young man seized control of
Milan, disinherited Bernabo's children, and imprisoned his uncle
and wife in the castle of Trezzo. The incident, which took
everyone by surprise, shook the political scene in the whole of
the north. It was all the more surprising as young Giangaleazzo
was considered by all to be a lily-livered young man. He kept pet
leopards and enjoyed reading books from his father's library.
To the outside world he appeared more concerned with
intellectual pursuits than politics and warfare. No one had hitherto
considered him a threat of any kind in the balance of milanese
power, let alone capable of dislodging his tyrannical uncle who
had ruled the milanese states for so long.

  News of the incident reached far flung shores including
England where it was recorded by Chaucer in the Monk's Tale:

> *Of Milan greate Bernabo Viscounte*
> *God of delight, and scourge of Lombardye*
> *Why should I not thine infortune recounte,*
> *Sith in estaat thou clombe were so hye?*
> *Thye brother son, that was thy double allye,*
> *For he thy nevew was, and son-in-law,*

Within hisprison made thee to die,
But why, ne how, noot I that thou were slawe

Carlo Visconti, Hawkwood's brother in law, immediately fled out of harm's way to Cremona, whence he wrote to Hawkwood appealing for help. By now almost ten years on from his marriage, Hawkwood was not on the best of terms with his father-in-law, Bernabo. He paid no heed to Carlo's appeal. Instead, on hearing of the incident, he rushed off to Milan to do fealty to Giangaleazzo, to whom he pledged the services of 30 lances for the hefty fee of 300 florins a month and a premium of 1,000 florins. He refused the many entreaties of the family to help rescue and reinstate the wretched Bernabo who, not long afterwards, died in captivity.

At this stage neither Hawkwood nor Florence appeared to realise the full intentions of the young upstart Giangaleazzo, and still considered him harmless. Hawkwood, partially on account of his wife, and more importantly as an agent of the english crown, was diplomatically trying to keep in with all sides. Moreover he needed the money. In reality young Giangaleazzo was already dreaming and scheming of extending milanese domination over the whole of the north of the peninsula. Having taken this political precaution, Hawkwood returned to the relative peace of Montecchio. There he contented himself with country life, interspersed by local skirmishes largely consisting of menacing the Sienese. We hear nothing of substance about his military activities until 1387.

Defence of Padua

In January of 1387, with the blessing of Florence, Hawkwood
allied himself with the paduan Cararras of Pavia in their defence
against the Venetian backed veronese Scaligers of Verona who had
been menacing them with their superior strength for some time,
and between whom no love had ever been lost. No doubt the
agreed fee was appealing, and Hawkwood may have felt some

loyalty to Padua whom Florence had previously befriended in the
1370s. Even with Hawkwood and his troops the allies were far
outnumbered by the Veronese who had 9000 men at arms and
2,600 archers together with a multitude of hastily mustered
citizens, as opposed to the allies 7,000 men and 600 archers.
    The Veronese tried every trick in the trade. First they sent
a spy disguised as an envoy purporting to treat for peace with
young "Novello", the nickname of Francesco Carrara,
the paduan general and son of King Ramiro, who was known as
"il Vecchio". Hawkwood promptly imprisoned the spy and
retreated the allies to a place called Cerea where they narrowly
missed being killed by the poisoned wine that awaited them.
This Hawkwood is purported to have detoxified by the insertion
in the chalice of his gold ring. This story, whether true or
apocryphal, illustrates the charisma which the English knight

exercised. Having refreshed themselves without fear of death, Hawkwood ordered the the troops to report to their standards. Then invoking Saints Prosdocimus, Anthony, Justinia and Daniel, mounted on a thessalonian charger, he led his men away from their entrenchments beyond the canal of Castagnaro seemingly giving the pursuing enemy every advantage of attack.

Thinking the Paduans were retreating the Veronese were greatly surprised to find them lined up for attack on the further banks of the canal thus blocking their foothold. Due to their superior numbers the Veronese gradually did manage to break their ranks. However as soon as the enemy began to yield ground Hawkwood made a surpirse attack from the flank with a company which he had cunningly kept in reserve. By using skilful defencetactics the allies of this English knight were successful in overcoming the Scaligers taking over 5,000 prisoners, killing over 700 and wounding 840 whilst losing the relatively small number of 100 of their own men. These statistics indicate Hawkwood's preference for capturing the enemy as opposed to outright slaughter.

A 19th century inscription recording the Paduan defeat of the Veronese under the command of John Hawkwood is to be found on the surviving bell tower at Castagnaro. This battle must rank as the greatest victory of Hawkwood's military career, which at the age of 70 was no mean achievement.

Hawkwood's efforts went unrewarded by the Paduans. The booty gained from the enemy camp, the supply train and the 40 munition carts had to be shared out amongst the allies.

Florence did intervene to ensure Hawkwood his fee.

How Hawkwood reacted to what was seemingly such an unsatisfactory denouement to his triumph is unrecorded, but he had no interest in power, and once paid off, had no political affiliation with his erstwhile ally so probably did not harbour hurt feelings or pride.

Giangaleazzo Visconti who had been quietly observing the battle through the eyes of his spies in the neighbourhood now formed an alliance with the Venetians and took over lame and defeated Verona. Together they moved in to Padua forcing the Carraras to abdicate and flee.

Hawkwood was re-elected Captain General of Florence In the spring of 1387 for the useful fee of 500 florins a month and retired to Montecchio for the summer. Presumably he was always on call but no military activities of note are recorded till the following year.

Two timing

In 1388 Hawkwood was comissioned by Florence to defend her territories against the papal troops of Urban VI. After a very brief period this impulsive and obstinate roman pope had made himself very unpopular throughout the peninsula and was quickly nicknamed "inurbino" meaning the rude one. An antagonistic sonnet against Urban which was written at the time "in the ancient Castle Keep of Borgo Sansepolcro", spread throughout tuscany over the appenines from the upper Tiber valley.

The pope, not content with the sovereign responsibilities given him by his position as head of state and of the church, now took it upon himself to look for new interests in the Kingdom of Naples. He prepared to invade the *Reame* with large numbers to back the young Angevin heir, Louis, against the Florentine backed heir of the Hungarians, Charles Durazzo. For this purpose he removed himself from his seat at Lucca to where he had retreated and set out for Perugia. Here he began recruiting as many men of arms without employment as he could muster.

Florence was anxious to protect her own position as an independent state, which she felt was best preserved by maintaining a balance of power between the small and middle rank nobility in the papal lands. Hawkwood was well positioned to monitor the situation on her behalf from his fortress at Montecchio and did manage to intervene by aiding the passage of Vanni Vechietti to negotiate between Florence and the Pope.

The White Company, whose loyalty towards the Pope had increased dramatically, requested Hawkwood to be their Captain in this attack on Naples. This arrangement might have placed him in an awkward position with Florence, to whom he was affiliated and by whom he was paid, but it seemed that Hawkwood, in true mercenary spirit, entertained no such qualms! Undeterred he asked Florence for leave of absence to take up this position. Stranger still, consent was forthcoming "as long as the allies of Florence were not injured."

Meanwhile Carlo Visconti, Hawkwood's brother-in-law, had arrived in the neighbourhood longing to persuade Hawkwood to join with him to take revenge on his nephew, the erstwhile "lily-livered", Giangaleazzo. Florence by now had begun to realise the colour of the young man's spots, and was becoming increasingly nervous of his intentions. An emissary wa sent to Hawkwood with letters from Florence to try and persuade him to stay close at hand because *relations between Lombardy and Tuscany are developing in such a way that the outcome you have long hoped for will soon be implemented* [ie getting the better of Giangaleazzo]. *Your staying here will soon benefit both you and your friends. Rather* argued Florence *instead of going to the kingdom of Naples you should seek to detach Otto of Brunswick and make him a partner, because, together you would do great deeds, considering the valour of Messr Otto and the enmity which he feels towards the Conte di Virtu* – As Giangaleazzo was known. based on the French county of that name which he had conquered.

Hawkwood for the moment turned a blind eye to these entreaties as he felt the hour had not yet come. He moved slowly towards the south and eventually arrived at Capua. Here he did join forces with Otto of Brunswick to try and seize the crown of the *Reame* from Louis d`Anjou. Despite initial success the allies ultimately were forced to surrender Naples to Anjou leaving them no option but to retreat.

The vipers strike

Whilst still engaged in the south in the spring of 1389 Hawkwood received an urgent summons from Florence to return north where the menaces of the Conte di Virtu were becoming alarming. Having secured Verona, Padua and Ferrara the Conte di Virtu was now probing into Emilia and attempting to strangle Florence by cutting off her trade routes. Florence began to panic. Hawkwood did not comply with this summons immediately but insisted on waiting until he had secured promises of further remuneration. The terms were concluded, in July of that year, and without more ado, Hawkwood turned tail and returned, presumably to Montecchio. Here he fell to attacking the Sienese for their alleged support of di Virtu. For political reasons Florence officially stood back from this fray whilst privately encouraging Hawkwood in his endeavours to the extent of sending an engineer on standby to cut off the water supply from the Sienese if necessary!

In all these military assaults one has to remember, as Hawkwood pointed out to the well meaning Friars at Montecchio, that soldiers starved in times of peace. The only way they could survive was by plunder. As a general of the time his aim was to keep his troops fighting as much as possible in order to earn their daily bread which otherwise would have been very hard and expensive to come by.

Hawkwood did not entirely reign supreme in Tuscany.

There was a rival company under another English commander, John Beltoft. The aforesaid was secretly allied to the Conte diVirtu,who favoured Pope Urban's ambitions in the kingdom of Naples and hoped to distance the mercenary companies from tuscany where otherwise they might be engaged by Florence against him. Beltoft attacked Pisa from which he eventually extracted 13,000 florins to retreat. The Conte di Virtu also hoped through Beltoft to break up Hawkwood's company which was committed to remain in the service of Florence. Although Beltoft did not succeed in so doing, he did persuade Hawkwood to accompany him to the aid once more of Otto of Brunswick in December 1389.

Together the two companies set off south. They did not get further than Apulia Gaeta when relations between Florence and the Conte di Virtu became so strained that, finally recognising the danger that an expansionist Milan would threaten, Florence re-summoned Hawkwood to the Republic and declared war against her northern agressor. This in fact was the moment Hawkwood had been waiting for. With the speed and energy of a youngster he fought his way north. In order to deceive the opposition he laid a false trail by taking the longer route via the Maremma and Volterra. He completed the journey of eighty-five miles from Grosseto to Florence in just three days, twice the average speed of a medieval army! Florence took the unprecedented step of giving him a years contract, as opposed to the usual six months, and ordered him north.

The vipers struck

In May 1390 Hawkwood set out north with a force of 5,000 horsemen and 15,000 footsoldiers, in those days a powerful army indeed. His first success was to catch the Milanese in the tail as they were starting to withdraw from Bolognese territory. Although not a great victory it did give his troops a psychological boost. It also caused Ferrara to abandon the Visconti alliance and allowed the Carrara family to retake Padua from which they had been ousted by Giangaleazo three years previously. Hawkwood proceeded via Parma as far as the shelter of the, now friendly, city of Padua where he wintered his troops. Here he awaited the outcome of Florence's diplomatic negotiations with the French and Germans for a joint attack against the Visconti. By the spring of 1391 these negotiations were completed and the allies were ready for their move on Milan.

Hawkwood proceeded with his troops in a westerly direction from Padua and quickly reached the river Adda thirty miles short of Milan where he halted to await news of the German and French contingents who were to join him. Here, alas, things began to go horribly wrong. He waited and waited with no signs of either ally on the horizon. Eventually it was learned that the Germans under the Duke of Bavaria had been bribed by Giangaleazzo to withdraw. As for the French under Armagnac, they continued to prevaricate and their promised help never materialised. This caused a major crisis amongst the Florentine force as without the promised allied troops they had no chance of victory. Although the city of Milan was in a state of panic at the proximity of the enemy, Hawkwood knew he was greatly outnumbered and that his lines of communication were stretched to breaking point. For Hawkwood, with his troops rearing to go and having so nearly reached his goal. he was faced with a difficult decision. He appreciated that he had no realistic option but to conduct a fighting withdrawal. The situation had all the makings of a deep humiliation for Hawkwood and his men.

Such was the calibre of this English Knight that he was able to turn a defeat into a triumph which earned him more fame than his greatest victories. He force marched his men without any losses across the rivers Oglio, Mincio and Adige and finally the Po to the Arno valley. The retreat however was not without incidents. The most dramatic of these was crossing the river Adige where the Milanese had broken the river banks thus flooding the plain. In order to avoid the whole army being drowned, Hawkwood led the cavalry and footsoldiers to a crossing ten miles below the breach in the middle of the night.

The speedy and disciplined manoeuvre of an army, especially in withdrawal, was something unknown in 14th century Italy and became a subject of great astonishment and admiration, as a veritable masterpiece of medieval warfare. First of all it would never have been possible to discipline such a large contingent of indigenous troops who, as we have already noted, lacked the team spirit of their English counterparts. Secondly the English were hardier than their opponents who would not have easily been persuaded to forge their way across four rivers unaided! The stratgegy of Hawkwood's retreat was compared by contemporaries to the most brilliant of ancient Rome.

Meanwhile the Milanese had intercepted and defeated the French troops of d'Armagnac. Now thinking all Florence's defence contingents to be absent from the city they decided to attack Florence from the south. To their great surprise Hawkwood, hastily summoned back by the Republic, was swiftly on the spot to protect its frontiers, completing the journey in five days averaging thirty miles a day compared to the normal twelve to fifteen. Hawkwood found the Milanese were camped at Poggio a Caiano ten miles from Florence. With his troops he stealthily marched along the south bank of the Arno, which he crossed at Signa making a camp at Tizzana. Here with the help of Florentine aid he blocked the route of the Milanese to the city. Realising they had been outwitted the milanese general, Del Verme, began retreating his troops over the mountains – to him unknown ground. With his local knowledge and by using a short cut Hawkwood's 3000 lances were able to catch up with the Milanese, killing 2400 and taking 200 prisoners. Del Verme escaped but his army was routed.

Although Hawkwood had failed to take Milan his performance did make Giangaleazzo realise that he must make further preparations before thinking of seriously annexing Tuscany.

This was Hawkwood's last campaign and as brilliant as any he had undertaken. Recognition of his services came at once from the City Fathers who awarded him a new tax free annuity of 2000 florins; a dowry of 2000 florins each for his daughters and a pension of 1000 florins for his widow provided, she did not remarry or leave Florentine territory after his death. In addition his male descendants were also granted Florentine citizenship.

Hawkwood retired to his house in the suburbs of Florence at Polverosa – for once in his life to rest on his laurels.

Finale in the Duomo

Interwoven in his career Hawkwood had always kept in touch with the English Sovereign, whose interests he carried, and with his estates at Sible Hedingham. By 1394, with his daughters safely married and at last feeling his age, he yearned to return to his native Essex to end his days. The notes of the Signoria remain which tell us: *"considering that Hawkwood was weary by reason of his great age, and as he states, incapacitated by infirmity, he desires to retire to his old country and to convert his annuity."* However Hawkwood was never able to fulfil this last wish as on March 16th 1394 this long lived old warhorse finally succumbed to an unexpected fit of apoplexy and died.

The City of Florence gave him a state funeral. His bier covered in cloth of gold and crimson velvet, accompanied by banners and wax torches ,was borne in procession to the Baptistery where it lay in state for some days to enable the public to make their last farewells. On the day of the burial the body was carried into the Duomo. It was attended by all the great and powerful of the city. A public holiday was declared and all the shops were closed on order. The cost of over 410 florins was approved by the Signoria without demur and they even paid for the widows weeds. The City had also promised him an imposing tomb in the Duomo but in the event, as was often the case at the time, this promise never came to fruition. Moreover a request was received from the English King Richard II that Hawkwood's body should be repatriated. Richard was known for his fascination with old bones and had successfully interceded with the upgrading of burial grounds for servants and friends. Taken in this context his request is not unusual. The Florentine reply was a masterpiece of diplomacy pointing out that:" *despite the fact that Hawkwood's glory was gained in* **their** *service and that he had been interred at* **their** *expense in the principal church of* **their** *city, they would accede to the English King's request so that it shall not be said that your Sublimity has uselessly and in vain demanded something from our Humility.*" The outcome is still a matter of conjecture and his remains have never been found either in Italy or England.

When the plan for the Florentine tomb was abandoned it was decided by the Signoria of Florence to create some alternative memorial to her English hero. To this intent two artists Agnoli

Gaddi and Giuliano d'Arigghi were commissioned to execute a fresco on the wall of the Duomo. Unfortunately no record of it survives. Forty years later, in 1436, this had fallen into disrepair. It was then that Paolo Ucello was commissioned to replace the old work. He decided to execute the new fresco against a dark green ground *terra verde*, with the image of an equestrian group in profile to simulate a marble funerary monument. His first attempt was not accepted, criticised for portraying too much of the horses belly and accompanying attributes. The second attempt was the masterpiece we see to-day. This trompe l'oeil of an equestrian group was a new creation in the vocabulary of art at that time. Unwittingly Hawkwood had given to the world, through the genius of Ucello, the earliest inspiration to re-invent the classical form of bronze equestrian monuments, as used in ancient Rome, attested to by the surviving statue of Marcus Aurelius on horseback which had recently come to light. This art form was brought to fruition by Donatello with his overlifesize bronze group of *Gattamelata* in Padua executed ten years after the fresco between1447-53, and subsequently by Verrocchio in his magnificent statue in Venice of the General Colleoni, of 1483. "The equestrian group" was subsequently adopted by painters and sculptors as an art for years to come.

Aftermath

Hawkwood's death left his widow Donnina alone in Florence in what she probably rightly feared would be difficult circumstances. She was by now thirty, although not old in our books considered middle-aged in the fourteenth century. In his latter years her husband had been haunted by debt and forced to surrender his properties to the state, including Montecchio, only a month or two before he died. The cunning Florentines by giving Hawkwood the great privilege of honorary citizenship also thereby made him liable for local taxes which, like today, were very high A further drain on his resources had been the marriages of his daughters. As is the custom today Italian weddings were of significant importance to the standing of the family. For any cuts in cost to be made would incur immense loss of face. There is further evidence of the collapse of a business deal whereby Hawkwood had placed 7,300 florins on deposit with a certain banker from Lucca, Alderigo Antelminelli, who proved unable to pay his creditors through what misadventure we know not. A mercenary's job sounds like a large money spinner, especially when you read the high sums Hawkwood extracted from the tuscan states for their protection. This does leave open the question as to where all the money went. Of course the troops had to be paid and in this Hawkwood was always scrupulous, unlike others in the business. His properties must have taken some upkeep and undoubtedly financial control was not his forte.

As Donnina must have been fully aware, all during his long years in Italy her husband had regularly sent back substantial funds to London where his affairs were looked after by a network of business contacts. It is only comparatively recently in 1930, under a pile of dusty documents in London's Guildhall Library, two important missives from Hawkwood to Thomas Coggeshalle came to light which give us an insight into his English affairs. The first of these dated 1392 was carried to England by Hawkwood's squire John Sampson by way of a letter of introduction from Hawkwood praying his old friend:

"to help and counsel his much loved squire John Sampson in those matters which he is pursuing for me at this time, namely for my safe conduct, and with regards to my will and my intent.... and also beg you to speak to Hopky Rykyngdon and to John Sargeant, Robert Lyndeseye and all my other friends that they do as John Sampson tells you regarding my will. Trusted friend may the Holy Ghost guard you."

Unfortunately Hawkwood left no official will but his intentions were made very clear in the indenture drawn up by John Sampson in the following year. This document reveals the extent of the estate Hawkwood had built up in England during his absence abroad and goes some way to explain his dearth of funds in Italy:

"My master Sir John Hawkwood greets you warmly and informs

you that he intends to come to England, and I have come to obtain two safe-conducts, one for my master and another for myself and five men and five horses, and therefore will I go again to Calais at the time that all these lords are there. And also my master has asked me to tell you that if he should die before he returns home that you should know what he desires to be done with the lands and tenements that have been purchased on his behalf in England. the which he has entailed for his daughters in Italy. Firstly he wishes that the Leadenhalle, together with the advowsons of the Church be sold. And that a chantry of two priests be founded in the convent of Castle Hedingham to sing there in my master's chapel, and one priest in the parish of Sible Hedingham. And also if my Lady Hawkwood outlives my master Sir John Hawkwood and, the Lord protect her, comes to England, he prays you and all the other trustees to settle on her in her lifetime the grant to Liston's and Hostages [houses] in Sible Hedingham: to revert thereafter to her son John Hawkwood intail. And the remainder of his estate should be held by his trustees until John my master's son has come of age. And when he comes of age the said grants should be settled on him and on his natural heirs; and should he remain without issue, the forementioned lands should be sold for the benefit of my master's soul and his friends' as you think best: and namely for the souls of those who were slain for his love. And in the time that my master's son comes of age that the profits of the lands also be set aside for the benefit of my master's soul and if my master comes home, as I hope he shall, then he will make his own arrangements *as he sees fit. This is written by me, the foresaid John Sampson at the Newhall in Boreham in Essex the 20th day of April, in the sixteenth year of our lord the King Richard [1393]."*

The revelations of this document are several fold. It confirms Hawkwood's wish to return to his native land, which sadly he never achieved. It portrays him as a man of deep religious conviction with much care for his fellow men – not the diabolical Englishman some would have us believe. It shows that the extent of his English estate was quite substantial with the fascinating reference to Leadenhall in London. Whether Donnina ever actually came over to England to assert her rights is uncertain. However she certainly made every effort to claim them as is evident in the petition she submitted to King Richard II requesting him to investigate the apparent embezzlement of her husband`s investments. As a result the kings Council instructed the then Lord Mayor of London Richard [Dick] Whittington to appoint a jury to look into Donnina's cause. Various witnesses were called to testify and confirmed that Hawkwood had bought a tenement called "Leadenhalle" in the parish of St. Peter with a part of the money,viz. 1200 marks, to the use of John Hawkwood... The deeds with other documents had been kept in a box of muniments belonging to Hawkwood placed for safe custody in St. Pauls Church. Alas by the time of the enquiry the box had mysteriously disappeared. Leadenhall was eventually sold in 1409 to Dick Whittington and others for £566 13s.4d, who sold it a year later to the mayor and commonalty, who still own this site as the Corporation of the City of London. To be fair the proceeds were used to endow the chantry Hawkwood had requested in St. Peter`s Church in Sible Hedingham which is still visible to-day.

How different are the two memorials a thousand miles apart; one of the Christian, in the rural anglosaxon village church, pleading to be remembered favourably by the Mother of God; the other of the benevolently portrayed military general lauding his skills as a leader and a soldier in the grandest renaissance cathedral of its time in northern Italy. This combination perhaps gives the true picture of the man: one who, despite the many bloody deeds, never lost his faith, his loyalty to his sovereign and his compassion for humanity. In the context of the time in which he lived and the profession in which he was engaged he stands out as a soldier of great skill, a fair leader of men and always true to his employer of the moment.

As for Donnina she appears to have returned to the city of her birth where according to a notary's document in 1399 she is recorded as living in a parish of Milan called *San Pietro in Camminadella*. She also appears to have recovered her rights to some of her dowry possessions including the castle of Pessano. Her daughters having all fled the nest she was only left with her son John, aged twelve at his father's death. He appears to have inherited none of Hawkwood's military aspirations. On reaching maturity in 1406 he returned to England where he was officially naturalised as a British subject, and found amongst his father's friends the support they appear to have denied his mother. He took over the management of the Essex estates, married and English girl and settled down to English country life. Sadly he and his wife remained childless so the male line of Hawkwood passed away. There do remain descendants through the female line, the progeny of Beatrice, third daughter of Sir John Hawkwood and his first wife, who married John Shelley,the reputed ancestor of the poet percy Bysshe Shelley, around 1423.

Giangaleazzo Visconti was finally subdued in 1392 when a peace treaty was signed between Florence and Milan in Genoa. For all his aggression Milan had gained nothing at the end of the day, whereas Florence, thanks to Hawkwood`s numerous intercessions, emerged in a stronger and more powerful position than ever before.

*   *   *   *   *   *   *   *

NOTES

Through the accident of history Hawkwood's years in Italy straddled the threshold of what became known as the Renaissance, or in Italian as the Rinascimento. After the sackof the city in 476 and throughout the Middle Ages Rome had experienced a period of great misery. She was invaded several times both by Goths and Saracens and shaken by revolutions and internecine wars. Amongst all this the remains of its classical civilisation fell into ruins, and its religious artefacts were largely destroyed both through negligence and the disapproval of the Christian Church. With the gradual arrival of Greek philosophers in Florence in the 14th century there grew up a revival of interest in classical texts hitherto considered pagan and offensive to Christianity. This new interest led to the acquisition by the rich and enlightened of ancient manuscripts, and the formation of private libraries under the guidance of scholars and writers such as that made by the poet Petrarch for Galeazzo Visconti. This change of attitude was furthered by the return to Rome from Avignon of the papacy in 1376 under Gregory XI. The revival of interest in the arts and sciences led to the restoration and exploration of ancient monuments and architecture. A new city arose.

ITALIAN ARTISTS AND SCULPTORS WHO FLOURISHED DURING HAWKWOOD'S SOJOURN IN THE PENINSULA

Andrea da *Firenze* [1343-77] decorated the Spanish Chapel S. Maria Novella, Florence·/*Bonaventura Berlinghieri* the best known of one of three artist brothers, born in Lucca who flourished 1235 – 124

Camaino, Tino di [c1285-1337] Sienese sculptor largely of tombs who worked in Pisa, Florence and Naples.

Cavallini (1273-1330) worked in Naples for Angevin Kings – precursor in style of Giotto.

Cimabue[1240-60] Etruscan born but worked in Siena. His name was "Cenni di Peppi" but he is known by his nickname which translates as "oxhead". He was a contemporary of Dante who mentions him in his his Divine Comedy. He discovered and was the master of Giotto. He is famous for being one of the first artists to introduce beauty and expression of human form into his depiction of sacred personages, hitherto represented in the iconic Byzantine style.

Coppo di Marciovaldo [1225- c 1276]. A Florentine soldier captured at the battle of Montaperti who remained in Siena after the battle and turned his hand to painting. A surviving work is a crucifix in the duomo at Pistoia. He is credited with Guido di Siena as co-founder of what is known as the Sienese School of painting. This group of artists, with the backing of the rich Sienese merchants of the time, fused Italian and Byzantine styles with the introduction of elegance into late gothic art.

Cosmati – sculptor who worked in making inlaid floors, amongst which is one in Westminster Abbey in London. Born in the 1100s his workshop continued till 1300 .

Daddi, Bernardo [d 1348]   Painter of gold ground panels,   regarded as the outstanding painter in Florence after Giotto's death.

Duccio di *Buoninsegna* [1278-1318] He was the leader of the Sienese School of painting. The greatest artist of his time, his major extant work is his altarpiece made for the cathedral in Siena known as 'the Maesta'.

Gaddi, Taddeo [1300-66] Florentine painter alleged to be Giotto's Godson. His best known works are the frescoes in the church of Santa Croce.

Giotto di Bondone, [1267-1337], "Giotto " the Florentine shepherd boy discovered by *Cimabue,* who became the most innovative painter and architect of his time. Following in his master's footsteps he expanded the painted image to include, and imbue with dignity, figures from his daily life in the fields into religious scenes. He is also the first recorded artist to introduce space and depth into pictorial images. Among his best known works are the campanile of the duomo in Florence, and the frescoes in the Scrovegni Chapel in Padua.

Giotto's disciple *Ugolino di Nerio* [fl1317-27] known for his altarpiece in Santa Croce, Florence.

The *Lorenzetti* brothers [1320-1348] *Pietro,* and *Ambrogio* who is the author of the famous fresco series representing the Good and Bad Government in the town hall of Sien

Lorenzo Monaco [c.1370-c.1425] born Piero di Giovanni in Siena.   In1395 he joined the Camoldelese order in Florence and took the name of Lorenzo.   Hence he was known as "Laurence the monk". Famous for his altarpieces he was one of the late masters of the school of painting which became known as "International Gothic".

Margarito di Arezzo, [fl.c.1262] one of the earliest artists to sign his pictures. He worked largely in his native town of Arezzo.   He is represented in the London National Gallery

Martini, Simone di [1285-1344] Next to Duccio the most distinguished painter of the Sienese school. Regarded as his best work is 'The Annunciation' gold ground panel, now in the Uffizi Museum in Florence. Among other works he painted a portrait of Petrarch's muse, Mona Laura, which although now lost is mentioned in one of the poet's sonnets. Martini probably died of the plague.

Orcagna,Andrea [1308?-1368] Born *Andrea di Cione* he became known by his nickname *Orcagna* which was local slang for *arcangelo*. He was the leading Florentine artist of the third quarter of the 14th century, one of the few who managed to survive the Plague. Capomaestro of Orvieto Cathedral from 1358-62, he was a painter, sculptor,architect and poet. He was summoned by Pisa to paint a Last Judgement on the walls of the Campo Santo which includes a figure of Ugoccione della Faggiuola of Arezzo holding his nose to avoid the smell of putrid bodies! This work was a reference to the Plague. Florence commissioned him to decorate Loggia dei Lanzi built to shelter townsfolk in bad weather but unfortunately it was badly sited as it receives the full strength of wind! He was also commissioned by Florence to decorate the Church of Or San Michele built on the site of a grain market, which acquired large treasures resulting from donations received as votive offerings to stem the mortality rate of the plague. The church is notable for Orcagna's Tabernacle Group, made of stone simulating one block of marble, which was acclaimed a foremost work of the period. In his work Orcagna stuck to the format of Byzantine art.

Pisano, Nicolo [d1278/84] and his son *Giovanni* [d.after d1314] were the greatest sculptors of their period and the first to liberate the art of sculpture from the rude Byzantine style of the Greeks. Nicolo came

from Apulia where Emperor Frederick II had already encouraged
a classical revival. Both of them worked in the Duomo of Pisa.
Niccolo created the magnificent pulpit in the Baptistery c. 1300 and
Giovanni that in the Duomo where he startled onlookers by
introducing scenes from antiquity in his composition in a much freer
style than hitherto known. These scenes must have been inspired
partially by the ancient sarcophagi, brought as spoils to the city, which
had been left lying around in the Campo Santo. The most famous of
these scenes is that of the chase of Meleager and the Calydonian boar
placed in the façade of the cathedral. Niccolo also created the Fountain
outside the Duomo in Perugia. Giovanni designed the façade of Siena
Cathedral; and the pulpits for S. Andrea in Pistoia and for Pisa
cathedral.

Spinello Aretino [fl.1373-1410] Although from Arezzo he probably
trained in Florence. He was the most prolific muralist of his time. He
died in Arezzo aged 92.

ITALIAN ARTISTS AND SCUPTORS BORN DURI NG HAWKWOOD'S SOUJOURN WHO FLOURISHED AFTER HIS DEATH

Fra Angelico [c.1395-1455] born "Guido di Pietro", a Domincan monk
whose lyrical works earned him the nickname 'Angelico'.

Bruneleschi [1377-1446]The architect who built the cupola of
Florence Cathedral.

Donatello [1386-1466] born "Donato di Betto Bardi". Known for his
monumental and realistic sculptures.

Fabriano, Gentile da [c.1370-1427]. Associated with the birth of the
International Gothic movement c1375

Ghiberti, Lorenzo [1378- 1455] the sculptor of the bronze doors of the

Baptistery in Florence. Ma*solini [1384–1443] with was responsible for the decoration of the Brancacci Chapel in Santa Maria el Carmine, Florence.

Massaccio [handwritten annotation above "with"]

Quercia, Jacopo della [1376–1438] Sculptor of the tomb of Ilaria del Carretto in Lucca Cathedral.

Sassetta, Stefano di Giovanni [c.1392–1450], an outstanding Sienese painter of the fifteenth century

Uccello,Paolo [c1397–1470] the author of the posthumous equestrian portrait of Sir John Hawkwood in the Duomo, Florence.

PLACES AND PEOPLE

FLORENCE – Early History. Originally a Roman settlement, the city became the seat of a Christian Bishopric around the 4th century. In 774 she was conquered by Charlemagne. Around 854 Florence and Fiesole united as one city. At the time the capital of Tuscany was Lucca ruled over by a Margrave. The most famous was the Countess Matilda who inherited the title from her brother and sister. She was a feisty lady remembered among other things for her military accomplishments and her intervention between the Pope Gregory VII and the Holy Roman Emperor Henry IV. In 1115 the then Margrave Henry chose Florence as his residence which thus became the capital of Tuscany. By 1155 the city had become a self ruling commune. Although by no means a dictatorship as officials were elected by lot. New outbreaks of political upheaval and division between the Pope and the Holy Roman Empire occurred in 1302 resulting in a period of instability which endured over the next thirty years.

SIENA had been a Ghibelline city since 1186 when Henry, the son of Frederick Barbarossa, laid siege to the town which was harbouring many refugees from the Guelph stronghold of Florence. After a setback in 1235 when Siena lost the towns of Poggibonsi and Montalcino to Florence it replaced the current government, up till then restricted to noblemen, by a council of twenty-four, twelve of whom were merchants. It became an important trade and business centre. In 1254 it occupied Pisa. Its moment of triumph was in 1260 when it gave a resounding defeat to Florence at Montaperti against a huge force of 40,000. Trade and culture flourished and it was this period which gave birth to the Sienese school of painting. This stability lasted till 1269 when it suffered a defeat at Monteriggioni. From then on the city began to slide towards guelph politics. Finally in 1287 it allied herself with Florence and set up a new Council of Nine, which excluded any members of the nobility. In 1355 the city was overthrown by the ghibelline supporters of the Emperor Charles IV. Subsequently it began to lose its political and economic power, aided and abetted by famines and the plague.

GUELPHS AND GHIBELINES. The names of these two factions arose from the dispute for power between the papacy and the Holy Roman Emperor. In 1077 Countess Matilda of Tuscany was the principal supporter of Pope Gregory VII in this controversy and was responsible for orchestrating the Emperor Henry IV's famous penance at her castle at Canossa where the pope was staying. Henry had to wait outside the castle for three nights in the snow dressed only in a cassock before the pope would receive him. The conflict between the twoparties continued over the years until, in theory, it was resolved by a concordat agreed between Pope Calixtus II and Emperor Henry V near the city of Worms in 1122 which ruled that the elections of bishops and abbots should be made by the proper ecclesiastic electors as opposed to secular rulers.

After the death of the Emperor Henry V however there followed a dispute of succession between the house of Hohenstaufen and that of Bavaria. The former were for the Emperor and against the Roman Church; the latter were for the papacy and promoted the election of bishop Lotario de Supplimburgo [1125–38] King of Saxony. This election was opposed by Conrad III of Swabia, and Federico di Hohenstaufen who were in favour of Cozzaolo III. The conflict between the two families should have been governed by the Concordat Instead the disagreement augmented the dispute on either side. Those in favour of the Emperor adopted the name of the Castle of Waibling – transcribed as *Guaibelinger* or Ghibellina and were known as *la parta nera* . The faction in favour of the papacy adoped the name of Welf – *Guelfo di Bavaria* or Guelf were known as *la parta bianca* Popular legend attributes the origin of the two nicknames to a famous feud over a young married woman between two rival brothers of Pistoia in 1215. After a heavy night of merrymaking over the Easter festivities the feud escalated into extreme violence. The two protagonists, were called Gualfredi who attained to *la parte bianca* of the city,and Guiglielmo who attained to *la parte nera*. The nickname of "Bianca" derived from name of the first wife of the Senator Cancelliere whose descendants adopted her name. The opposing faction took the contrasting name of "Nera". Despite overtures for forgiveness both brothers suffered bloody and gory deaths. Their names and story went down in history. The nicknames of *la parte bianca* and *la parte nera* were retained ever since by the Guelphs and Ghibelines. Giorgio Villani, on the other hand,sets the feud in Florence between the Bondelmonte supporters of the Emperor Charles IV. Both incidents are reported to have taken place over Easter in 1216

PETRARCH, Franceso [1304-1374]. The son of a notary at the papal court in Avignon, he begun life as a minor cleric. He soon turned his pen to poetry inspired by his muse and girlfriend, Laura, on whom he based much of his work, in particular his Canzoniere, a sonnet sequence in praise of a woman of that name. He became famous for his madrigals and songs written in the vernacular. In 1341 he was crowned Poet Laureate in Rome. By the 1360s he had moved to Pavia where he became an ornament of the Visconti court. He acted as unofficial secretary to both brothers and as literary adviser to Galeazzo.

Petrarch was the first scholar to explore the rhetorical and stylistic qualities of a range of neglected classical Roman writers such as the statesman and orator, Cicero, Livy and Virgil. He scoured libraries and monasteries for classical texts and in 1333 discovered a manuscript by Cicero *Pro Archia* where he compared rhetoric with oratory. In his famous speech *De Oratore* Cicero opined: ""both the diversity of their ways of life and the wholly opposed ends for which they have worked, make me believe that philosophers always thought differently from orators. For the latters efforts are directed toward gaining the applause of the crowd, whilst the former strive – if their declarations are not false – to know themselves, to return the soul to itself and to despise empty glory". Petrarch was known for the simplicity of his dress. He shunned costly court costumes preferring to wear the habit of a monk.

DEFINITION OF A KNIGHT

Professor Southern 1950s:High Theory: "to protect the Church, attack infidelity, reverence the priesthood, protect the poor, keep the peace, shed one's blood and, if necessary, lay down one's life for one's brethren."

Working knights:– it was thought enough " to defend one's rights, see justice done, keep one's inferiors and superiors in their place, be a wise counsellor and a bold fighter, a loyal vassal and a respected lord, and make the exercise of arms profitable." A knight was entitled to 4 horses; a Squire to 3 and an archer to 2.

PARDONS

Despite his good relationship with Edward III Hawkwood probably recognised that with the King's successor and his advisors this might be less friendly. He petitioned for" a *pardon "as the King has granted Sir Robert Knollys for God and Charity"*. On the 2nd March 1377 just before Edward III died the pardon was granted *"special at the asking of the nobles, magnates and commonalty of the realm, and for good service rendered in the King's wars of France and elsewhere."*

LETTERS

1374 TO THE PRIORS OF SIENA [T & M doc 19]:
Magnificent and powerful lords, and dearest friends
So that your magnificence should not be surprised, we are letting you
know that we had heard that a large company of men-at-arms was
gathering outside the boundaries of your territory in order to fight with
us, and for that reason we came here to find out if the facts
corresponded with reports.   As a result, if it pleases your lordships to
spend a certain sum of money on this company, as customarily ought to
be spent on men-at-arms, we will abstain from damage and, so far we
can, we will keep your territory free from harm but if not , we will
allow Pillagers from that company to do whatever they wish.   Let us
know your disposition in regard to these matters.
Hawkwood and Konrad Count Hechilberg Captains

CARLO VISCONTI to HAWKWOOD describing a coup:
To our magnificent, dearest, and closest friend
We are writing to tell you that today at high noon in Milan, the Lord
Count of /virtye has captured and imprisoned the magnificent and high
lord, his lord and our lord and father, together with our magnificent and
dearest brother and Lord, Luigi Visconti.   We ourselves are free, in
our citadel of Crema, and the fortress of Porta Romana is also holding
out in our name.   Accordingly, we affectionately ask you to show your
worth as a brother, by coming to our aid immediately via Parma, and
bringing with you any men-at-arms which you have yourself, or which
you can gather together from among your friends; and we have plenty

of money available, ready to be paid out in wages, according to your commands; but it is time for you to show your strength, in the way you know how, and as how you always used to do. Please reply immediately

Given at Crema on May 6th [1385]

AGREEMENT reached between Hawkwood and Gian Galeazzo Visconti on the latters suppression of Milan in 1385:

Be it known that Sir John Hawkwood, of England, knight , has promised and sworn to Franchishino de Caymis,proctor of Gian Galeazzo Visconti, Count Virtù, of Milan, and Martin, public notaries to observe faithfully all the following matters:

Firstly, if the said count requires his services, he promises to come, unless he is in the pay of some community or lord so that he cannot do so honourably, and even then he will be bound to serve, if the Count desires, at the expiry of his contract. On the other hand, the said proctor undertakes that if Sir John comes when required, the Count will give him a provision of 300 florins a month. Also Sir John may bring with him esquires up to thirty lances, to whom the Count will pay such wages as he is giving to the other esquires than in his service. if Sir John brings more than thirty, by the Count's order, they shall receive the same as other lances receiving wages from the Count. Moreover the Count shall not be bound to pay the 1,000 florin, which the said proctor offered to Sir John yearly, if he does not come and has not been prevented by just impedimemts, up to the fourth month after the request......

REFERENCES

BRUNI, Leonardo [1377–1444]: Assault of Faenza. *The English,
thanks to the incredible perversity of their leader, once inside the walls
inflicted everything on its citizens that is usually inflicted on stormed and
captured cities. For everything was laid open to pillage, the men were
either beaten or killed, the women raped, and things both sacred and
profane were wretchedly and impiously polluted by the cruelty of the
barbarians. Finally, when it had at last been stripped bare of
everything, leaving only the town walls and houses, the evil captain sold
the place itself to the rulers of Ferrara .*

BRUNI, Leonardo [1377–1444] Pope Gregory XI's reply to Florentine
Ambasdadors after sack of Faenza: *We are not tyrants, nor do we wish to
be. But we believe that citadels are relevant to the safety and utility of
peoples, to control them and keep them quiet, and so that unstable and
reckless men, of which cities are full, do not dare incite revolutions
contrary to the will of the good. With respect to your blaming the
governors for these revolts, it is quite obvious to us that none of these
peoples defected until they were driven to defect by your urgings and
promises, so that you, not our governors, are the cause of the revolts.
At the end of your speech you lament piteously the calamity of the
people of Faenza – but as though the origin of that calamity were not
the rebellion of Bologna! For the English would never have invaded
Faenza if Bologna had remained loyal. Thus,, those who were the cause
of the Bolognese rebellion are also the cause of the wretched destruction
of Faenza.*

CAVALCANTI[1381–1451] He [Hawkwood] *went most mornings toconsult with the Ten of War and, more often than not, it fell out that the said captain gave advice to the Ten instead of the Ten giving orders to him.*

CHRONICLER OF RIMINI: Cesena: *As many men, women and nurselings were found slaughtered, so that all the squares were full of dead, of both sexes. A thousand drowned in trying to cross the moats – some fled by the gates with the Bretons pursuing, who murdered and robbed and raped, and would not let the handsomer women escape, but kept them for* themselves.

DEUTERONOMY, ch.20. v10 and 13: *when thou comest near unto a city to fight against it, thou shalt offer it peace But if it will make no peace with thee thou shalt smite all the males thereof with the edge of the sword.*

DUGGAN, CHRISTOPHER The Force of Destiny, Penguin 2008, quotes Ugo Foscolo *Dell'origine e dell'officio della letteratura* inEdizione nazionale delle opera di Ugo Foscolo, Santini, Florence 1933:
"Oh, the virtues, misfortunes and errors of great men cannot be written in cloisters and ivory towers! O Italians I exhort you to the study of history, as no other people can more disasters to be lamented, more errors to be avoided, more virtues to be respected, and more great spirits worthy of rescue from oblivion".

HOLMAN, WILLLIAM Halstead, Essex. He probably received most of his information about the chantry in Sible Hedingham Church from thethen Rector Moses Cooke who wrote to him with the following description in1714: "*In the South wall of the Chantry the Executors of Sr John Hawkwood erected also an arched Monum[en]t of stone to his Memory, embellished with Wood-bine Leaves, several Hawks, the Wild Boar, Hare, & other inhabitants of the Wood, in Allusion to his Name: Within the Arch on the Wall in Colours are the Potraitures of Sr John Hawkwood & two Women [his 2 wifes, if Tradition may be regarded] standing in a devout Posture, their Hands lifted up & conjoined, with Sentences issuing out of th⟨ei⟩r Mouths & going over t[hei]r Heads in a Character agreeable to th[a]t Age viz over his Head "vere fili dei miserere mei" over the 1st Woman "[M]ater dei meme[n]to mei" and over the last "[Mater] xi meme[n]to mei".* Essex Record Office D/Y Moses Cooke to William Holman, 23.04.1713

MURIMUTH: *In that time, the Englishman Sir Hawkwood rose to prominence. He had the White Company with him, and fought now against the Church, now against the lords of Milan, and he did many extraordinary things, really marvellous things, the like of which no one had heard of before [mirabilia inaudita].* The Contination of Trivet and Murimuth's Chronicle, Oxford [1719-22]

SIENESE CHRONICLER: *Sir John Hawkwood, not to be held entirely infamous, sent a thousand of the Cesenese women to Rimini'*

WESTMINSTER CHRONICLE {1381-1394} Oxford Clarendon Press 198:*A squire who had for some time been in the company of Sir John Hawkwood in Lombardy arrived at the king's court with a story about a man of religion living in those parts, who predicted that within the ensuing three years the English nation, because of its evil life, would be mercilessly punished chiefly, so he said, by famine and pestilence, but* that after this the country would be the happiest of all Kingdoms

VILLANI, GIOVANNI [1300–1348]
DESCRIPTION OF ENLGISH SOLDIERS BEHAVIOUR

Very obedient to their commanders.....in matters of discipline....[but in their camps or cantonments, through a disorderly and over-baring boldness, [they] lay scattered about in great irregularity, and with so little caution that a bold resolute body of men might in that state easily give them a shameful defeat.

ROUTES AND TRAVEL

The routes used by Hawkwood and his companies were largely those created by the Romans in the first millennium AD. The chief of these roads were the Via Flaminia, the Via Arimensis, which stretched from Arezzo to Rimini, and the Via Emilia.

CRUSADES

1096 - 1099

1147 - 1149

1189-1192

1202 - 1204

1217 - 1221

1228 - 1229

1248 - 1254

1270 - 1271

BIBLIOGRAPHY

Balduzzi, Luigi, *Bagnocavallo e Giovanni Hawkwood in Atti e Mem.Storia Patria, Prov.Romagna*, Bagnocavallo, S.3rd II, 1884 p. 71

Ballestraci,Duccio; *Le armie, i cavalli, l'oro,* Rome 2003

Bartolomei, Giacomo, *Sigliano al confine della civilta delle alpe*, Cantagalli, Siena 1995

Beaver, Kinter; *A Tuscan Childhood, Viking, London 1993*

Bonazzi, Luigi, *Storia di Perugia*, 1860

Bondelmonti, M; *Giovanni Villani*

Borsook, Eve *L'Hawkwood d'Ucello et la Vie de Fabius Maximus*, Revue de l'art LV France 1982

Bruni, Leonardo Arezzo 1370– Florence1444, *Istoria Fiorentino.* Bruni was Chancellor of the Florentine Republlic 1427 –1444

Cavalcanti, Giovanni, *Istorie Fiorentine* 1381–1451, Florence 1821

Cole, Hubert, *Hawkwood in Paris; Hawkwood & Towers of Pisa*, Eyre & Spottiswoode, London 1967

Cook, Albert S. *The last months of Chaucers earliest patron*, Newhaven, Connecticut 1916

Corpus chronicorum bononiensium, ed. Lapi, Citta di Castello,1916

Cronache Senesi [I Ciompi] 1352

Cronichetta di Malatesti ,Faenza 1846

Froissart, Jean *Suite du livre Premier*, chaps mlxv, mlxv1, livre second chap 11

Gatari, Galeazzo and Gatari, Bartolomeo, *Cronaca Carrarese di Galeazzo e Bartolomeo, 1318–1407*

Gaupp, Fritz, History, *the Condottiere John Hawkwood* , March 1939

Giovio, Paolo,*; Elogia virorum bellica virtute illustrium*

Green, *John Richard, History of English People*, Macmillaln & Co, London 1895

Johnson, Paul, *Edward III;* Weidenfeld, London 1973

F.E.Halliday, *Chaucer & his world,* Thames & Hudson 1968

Hamilton, Olive, *Paradise of Exiles, Tuscany and the British*, Andre Deutsch 1974, p26

Maurice, John; *A life of John Hawkwood*, from Sir William Boswell's

[English Ambassador to the Hague] correspondence with J de Laeet, Leiden 1640–41

Minerbetti, Piero di Giovanni, *Cronica volgare di anonimo fiorentino,* 1385–1409

Murimuth, *The Continuation of Trivet and Murimuth's Chronicle, 2 vols,* Oxford ,1719–22

Pearsall,Derek *The Life of Geoffrey Chaucer* , Blackwell, Oxford 1992 pp.53, 107

Pellini, Pompeo, *Dell Hstoria di Perugia, Parte* 1, Venice 1654

Sardo. Ranieri, *Cronica di Pisa di Ranieri Sardo,*ed. O Banti, Rome 1963

Sacchetti, Franco, *Il libro delle Trecentonovelle* Ed Li Gotti, Milan 1946

Salzmann,L.F; *Building in England down to 1540* , Clarendon Press, Oxford 1952

Sercambi, Giovanni, *Le Croniche del Codice Lucchese,* Rome 1892

Speight, Historical *Background of Chaucer's Knight,* [trans. Conn. Academy of Art & Sciences] pp 182–6

Stefani, *Cronaca Fiorentina di Marchionne di Coppo Stefani, vol 11 1373–74*

Ricotti, *E. Storia delle Compagnie di Ventura in Italia,* Pomba,Turin 1845

Ritchie, Neil, History Today, *Sir John Hawkwood,* Oct 1977

Tabanelli, Mario, *Giovanni Acuto, Capitano di Ventura,* Faenza, 1975

Temple-Leader, John, and Marcotti, Giuseppe: *Sir John Hawkwood:Story of a Condottiere,* T. Fischer Unwin, London 1889

Trease, Geoffrey:*The Condottieri: Soldiers of Fortune,*London, 1970.p.148–9,

Tuchman, Barbara, *A Distant Mirror,* 1978, pp225, 254

Velluti, Donato, *La Cronica Domestica,* 1367–70, ed.I.del Lungo and G.Volpi Florence1914

Varese, Ranieri, *Storie della moda,* Calderini 1995

Villani, Giovanni, *Matteo,* Filippo;*Chroniche di Giovanni, Matteo e Filippo Villani,* Trieste,1858